£750
(m)
'A R÷W

PRE-1841 CENSUSES & POPULATION LISTINGS

IN THE BRITISH ISLES

Colin R Chapman

THIRD EDITION

LOCHIN PUBLISHING

This is another in the series of Chapmans Records Cameos designed to bring some of the less often used record sources to the attention of social, local and family historians world-wide. This cameo and others in the series by the author originated as his lectures, many of which are profusely illustrated with pertinent examples. The author will, accordingly, be pleased to lecture to family history, genealogical or other societies or groups on the subject of this cameo or other matters of interest to the social, local and family historian.

The cover illustration is adapted by Sarah Elliott from P Brueghel's 'The Numbering at Bethlehem' - one of the earliest recorded pre-1841 censuses - mentioned in the preface.

Published by
LOCHIN PUBLISHING
6 Holywell Road, Dursley, GL11 5RS, England

First Edition 1990 (1 873686 00 5)
Second (revised) Edition 1991 (1 873686 04 8)
Third (revised) Edition 1992
Copyright of the Lochin Publishing Society 1990,1991,1992

British Library Cataloguing in Publication Data
Chapman, Colin R. 1939-
Pre-1841 Censuses & Population Listings in the British Isles - 3 (rev) ed.
I. Title II.Series
304.6
ISBN 1 873686 06 4

LOCHIN
PUBLISHING
SOCIETY

Table of Contents

Preface

In 1973 the Bedfordshire Historical Record Society published a transcript of the 1782 census of Cardington, edited by David Baker. In my student days in chemical research I had been taught to pursue information indicated in bibliographies and to read references in full. It was reading the works quoted by Baker that inspired me to locate other similar censuses, enumerations, surveys and lists of people. Thus the journey on my quest began, fitted in around my many other commitments at that time, not the least of which were in my periods of office within the Federation of Family History Societies. I was able to reach the initial public milestone in my quest at the First British Family History Conference in 1980, appropriately at Bedford, when I gave a lecture on pre-1841 censuses - incorporating the Cardington census into my presentation. In my audience was Jeremy S W Gibson who immediately suggested I commit that lecture to paper for broader consumption.

At that time my diverse responsibilities did not permit my doing so; but I have been pleased to note that JSWG took up the challenge himself and personally followed many of the examples I quoted. With his unique enthusiasm he contacted or visited the various record offices around the British Isles for details of their holdings, culminating in not a few of the Gibson Guides, published by the Federation of Family History Societies. To JSWG I am, accordingly, grateful for drawing some early population listings to the attention of a wider audience than I or Baker, my guru in absentio, had originally considered.

Over the intervening years, however, I have acceded to many requests to deliver lectures on this topic to audiences all over the world. And during the period several individuals, many of them now firm friends, have planted further milestones in my quest by providing me with more lists of people prior to 1841. On very many occasions members of my audiences have repeated JSWG's original suggestion that I make my notes available in a more permanent format. It is in response to these requests that another milestone has been reached as I have prepared this cameo.

With my 1980 lecture as the framework and the numerous additional examples acquired in the last decade I have compiled the following account. I have been terribly unacademic and have unashamedly interwoven simple enumerations of people, even surveys and numbers of houses, with detailed listings which furnish names, ages, addresses, occupations, religious affiliations and more. Local unique lists are jumbled among national surveys, military with peaceful, and the ecclesiastical and civil are side by side. I have even tossed in a few taxation lists which affected only a small proportion of the community as I consider such lists are very much under-utilised as sources of names. My critics may protest; but I firmly believe that serious family historians will need to set their ancestors into the total context of the local, county and national situation. Hence even numbers can provide that additional gem to the polished family history. Whilst casual name collectors or pedigree producers may, therefore, find the following pages rather irritating, even they may discover some of the references useful in their specific searches. And here I must express particular thanks to the librarians of the University Libraries at Bristol and Birmingham and of the Royal Society of Chemistry, who have permitted me to spend many happy hours dipping into periodicals, stretching back over 200 years, to locate references to early population listings. The staff of the library at the British Museum - the British Library - have been equally patient in assisting me to understand the logic of their nineteenth century cataloguers. At the Guildhall Library, London, the staff have helped to locate some nineteenth century censuses of the City parishes. It is in tribute to these librarians that I have provided for readers of this cameo, who have similar curiosity to my own, detailed references - many scores of them - should they wish to read the original accounts.

I have followed a chronological sequence - after all that is how we enjoy our lives - rather than use a geographical or thematic ordering of events; indeed many a census was taken as a consequence of the success or failure of a preceding one, and to hop otherwise than in a successive pattern would lead to certain confusion. Thus to appease those who have not the patience or determination to examine every page of my text I have appended (in Appendix I) a county-by-county breakdown of the various censuses containing individuals' names with the dates of those censuses. I have expanded on many of the listings within the main text of this cameo. For completeness I have also appended (in Appendix II), but with little comment, a list of decennial censuses containing names of individuals from 1801 to 1831.

In my text I have failed to distinguish between enumerations which were de jure and those which were de facto - the former requiring people to return to their places of origin to be counted (as at the Nativity of Christ i.e. the Numbering at Bethlehem illustrated on the cover of this cameo), and the latter requiring the survey to be taken of the contemporary population in a particular place (the more common situation, as exemplified during the nineteenth and twentieth centuries). But I assume that such distinctions will be of little concern to the majority of my readers. In general I have arbitrarily reserved the term census to indicate a listing where names of people are included; and where only numbers are provided I have used the term enumeration. But I have occasionally lapsed from my own definitions in my enthusiasm to encourage researchers to consult original documents. Hopefully those who know me will be understandingly patronising in this regard.

I am aware that many local listings may exist further to those I have quoted on the following pages. Indeed, in this cameo I have concentrated on providing some examples of population listings within the British Isles which may be of value in historical research, or even of passing interest to the curious. Nevertheless, I would be delighted to be informed of other local listings, together with any notes on their original purposes, their present whereabouts or availability of copies which could be consulted by fellow researchers.

A complementary publication by Mervyn Medlycott, in association with Jeremy Gibson, is nearing completion. It will provide fuller lists of local census listings than in my appendices - but not their detailed backgrounds as I have described here.

COLIN R CHAPMAN.

1. 1841 - The ultimate census

1841 is regarded by many who are interested in British genealogical research as the beginning of an era - the first of the nineteenth century returns of use to the family historian. Names and occupations are quoted and ages given to the nearest five years (rounded downwards); the birthplace is stated as being within or outside the county of residence. Equally important, individuals are grouped together in households, each householder having filled in, probably with assistance, a separate schedule.

In reality, however, the 1841 census is more of an end product, the acme of campaigning and correspondence which had been pursued for decades, even generations. A major victory was achieved in 1800 when the principle of a national enumeration of the people was accepted in the Population Act by the parliament of that time. Many attempts had been made before the nineteenth century to persuade English monarchs and governments, and even the Church, to conduct a national census; Bills had been introduced into and laid before parliaments, but all had failed either because of lack of time to debate the argument, lack of finance to implement the aspirations or a total lack of support for the proposed legislation.

Even when the national, decennial census was introduced in England and Wales in 1801, the authorities neither requested nor required the names of individuals; the only information solicited was the number of males and females employed in agriculture; the number employed in trade, manufacture or handicraft; and the number not in either of these two categories. Although this system provided enumerations a certain amount of confusion arose as many women and children and servants were put into the third category, irrespective of their actual occupations. In an attempt to resolve these anomalies the 1811 and 1821 questionnaires requested the number of families in each category, and the results were published as numerical analyses by counties, hundreds, parishes, and townships or municipical boroughs.

The employment categories were extended from three to seven in 1831 and the category of trade and handicraft was further divided into specific occupations; these had to be indicated on the formula compiled by the local constable or overseer who conducted the enumeration. 1821 was the only occasion prior to 1841 when an age structure (albeit a crude one) was requested; and whilst in 1801 the numbers of inhabited and uninhabited houses were required, as in all subsequent censuses, the number of houses being built was not included as a question until 1811.

The Population Act of 1801 further required every incumbent to supply the numbers of baptisms and burials in his parish for both males and females from 1700 to 1780 and also for each year from 1781 to 1800; the number of marriages in each year from 1754 to 1800 was also required. The printed summaries of the enumerations published by central government, which are certainly worthy of study, include these parochial statistics by counties and hundreds and for the larger cities. In 1811, 1821, 1831 similar questions on vital statistics for the preceding ten years were asked , and in 1831 information on the ages of deceased persons from 1813 to 1830 and the number of illegitimate births was requested as well. Again, the printed summaries provide the numerical analyses of the results submitted.

Whilst the 1800 Act elicited only numbers of people, and the printed summaries contain the same data in an organised format, many enumerators made detailed listings of their local populations and included names, family groups and relationships, ages, even dates of birth, and added notes of immigration patterns into their parishes. Some early nineteenth century censuses thus provide similar, or greater, information than that available in the 1841 or even the 1851 returns. Prior to 1841, however, this information was not required by the authorities collating the data centrally and so it was not forwarded to London; consequently these detailed censuses, where they survive, are in a variety of locations. Some appear in parish registers of baptisms, marriages or burials, often on the inside of the front or back cover. Some returns appear in the account books of the overseers of the poor for a particular parish. Some are found within the churchwardens' accounts books. Some of these early nineteenth century census returns were recorded in notebooks used specifically for that purpose and are to be found in the parish chest with other parochial documents. Some of these records have found their way into county record offices; others into museums, into local reference libraries, or into borough archives. Others remained among the personal papers of the schoolmaster, overseer, churchwarden, or incumbent who conducted the census survey - and have gone the way of all such private papers: a few have survived and have been deposited in suitable archive offices; some are possibly retained even now in private hands; but the majority have perished, their value unrecognized by the custodians of such documents. Slowly, however, detailed nineteenth century census returns are being discovered, their presence recorded, and their content transcribed, indexed and published.

Some of the 1801, 1811, 1821 and 1831 censuses which list individuals by name and give other details are quoted in Appendix II. After 1831 the organisation of conducting the censuses was greatly improved. The 1836 Registration Act, which introduced civil registration with local registrars responsible through Superintendent Registrars to the Registrar General, identified more reliable individuals who could be called upon to administer the censuses as well as a framework through which subsequent censuses could be managed.

2. Listings to the sixteenth century

Although the 1800 Population Act initiated the holding of decennial censuses from 1801, which became more sophisticated as they developed through the nineteenth century, censuses had been taken long before this time, both in the British Isles as well as further afield. Enumerations were even more common, the numbering of the Children of Israel in 1200 BC being one of the earliest documented [1]. There is ample evidence that the Romans conducted a census every five or fourteen years; a good example is that of 5 BC. The one held by Governor Cyrenius in AD 6 almost led to open revolt as those involved objected to the prospect of being called into military service. However, such enumerations rarely included names of individuals; and although population numbers are of use to demographers and statisticians, alone they are of lesser value to the family historian. On the other hand, population statistics for a community in which named ancestors can be identified are a most useful source of data through which individuals can be visualised and depicted in their contemporary context.

One of the first censuses in the British Isles of which we have tangible evidence was the Domesday Survey of 1086. This was compiled by Norman clerks at the instruction of William I, who wanted to know the extent of the land he had conquered and how it was managed. Landholders were listed by name and an indication was given of their status - villein, bordar, or serf [2]. At this time landholders were invariably male, thus the Domesday census provides listings of adult males only.

From this date throughout the country very many returns were made of individuals for various purposes and by various authorities. Both Church and State, which in some eras were inseparable and almost indistinguishable (even if in other eras their policies were totally polarised), conducted surveys of the people, often for the purpose of raising revenue. Some surveys were locally organised and for specific areas, while others were implemented nationally. The originals of many of these early surveys are held in the Public

Record Office; not a few have been transcribed, translated and published by historical record societies and antiquarian or archaeological societies beginning late in the last century [3].

In 1181 a Saladin Tithe (sometimes referred to as a Moveables Tax) was imposed on individuals' personal estate - in contrast to their real estate. As the rate was calculated on one-tenth of the value of the possessions for urban dwellers and one-fifteenth for rural dwellers, this duty was also termed the One-tenth and One-fifteenth Tax by some authorities. In some parts of the country the actual value of the goods being assessed was declared and sworn as correct by the owners, in other areas jurors made the assessments. This tax remained on the statute books until 1623 although it was not enforced much after the medieval period.

From 1194 until 1224 the method of raising revenue reverted to assessments of real estate and a Hideage, Hidegeld or Carucage Tax was levied on each hide (or carucate) of land held. The division of land was based on the Domesday survey taken in the previous century.

Freemen's Rolls or Registers, such as those for the City of York from 1272, were maintained by Corporate Towns as a record of the names of freemen and guild members. Normally freemen were able to claim certain privileges in their borough or city, such as shares in the town's profits and exemption from tolls. Some of these registers have been transcribed and published by historical record societies, such as the 'Register of the Freemen of the City of York, Volume I, 1272-1558' edited by Dr Francis Collins for the Surtees Society [4].

The Statute of Winchester (1285) required every man between 15 and 60 to be assessed and sworn to arms according to his land and chattels (ie his real and his personal estate). The view of arms was to be made twice a year in each hundred and liberty by two constables; and when the justices visited the district the constables were to present any defaults. This was not innovative but confirmed an ancient Anglo Saxon Fyrd which had been developed by King Alfred to enable all men between 15 and 60 to serve their shire when called upon to do so; the motive was to prevent a repetition of the Danish invasion and so all possible fit and capable men were identified so they could be called away from their normal activities to help defend their locality. In reality calling men away from their places of work was likely to disrupt the local community and the local economy; thus the lists drawn up were likely to contain not all those between 15 and 60 capable of bearing arms, but those who could be spared locally. Thus any lists resulting from the Statute were by no means true censuses, and whilst at least two lists should have been made annually for each area, few appear to have survived. The Sussex listing in 1297 of ninety Gentlemen who were summoned to London for military service would seem to be a direct result of the 1285 Statute.

Between 1290 and 1332 sixteen [5] grants or subsidies were levied by the monarchs as methods of raising revenue. These were not annual taxes but were imposed as the need arose; accordingly, each subsidy was governed by the conditions laid down in the Act by which it was implemented. The normal rate of assessment was four shillings in the pound per annum on land worth twenty shillings and upwards, and two shillings and eight pence in the pound per annum on personal possessions worth three pounds and upwards. One, two or three subsidies might be granted by the same Act to bring in the necessary revenue, and payment could be spread over a year or more. The returns of those liable to pay were inscribed on parchment rolls and so commonly called Lay Subsidy Rolls. Unfortunately no British county has a complete set of these rolls, and there were many individuals who evaded payment whose names are thus unrecorded.

A further forty-two grants were levied between 1334 and 1434; but for these the wealth of each vill was assessed, so employing a different system from that of the earlier lay subsidies which used the wealth of individuals as the basis for the taxation. Thus the fourteenth century returns normally show the quotas for the villages only and do not name individuals. However, for Cornwall, Devon, Kent and Sussex, names are given. These lists provide a useful source of English surnames. The originals of these grants are held in the Public Record Office [6].

In 1377, 1379 and 1381 England suffered some crises as a result of wars, so further taxes were levied on all males over the age of fourteen. The taxpayers' names were recorded on poll tax lists for those years. Like the former lists, these are not true censuses since females and those under the age of fourteen are obviously missing and there were several evasions; but the names of those who did pay were recorded - normally in Latin, although those for Northumberland were in French. There was less evasion in 1377, when a flat rate of a groat per person was levied; this year is particularly useful to family historians for London, Carlisle, Colchester, Hull and Oxford. In 1379 and 1381 the rate was graded socially and the receipts, where they survive, contain the names of taxpayers and the amounts paid.

The 1488 list of resident males of Rye [7], Sussex, eligible to serve as constable or watchout for the town is one of the earliest local lists of names - but 1523 marks the year for the first census (in a form resembling that used in the nineteenth century) which has so far been discovered for anywhere in the British Isles. Part of the city of Coventry (ten wards) [8] was surveyed and a listing compiled of its inhabitants. The original census is held in Coventry by the city archivist.

The pretext of a muster to arms by counties and hundreds (see the 1285 Statute of Winchester) was used in 1522 to undertake a nation-wide valuation of properties. Some of the resultant Muster Lists and Rolls for several counties for this year have found their way into the Exchequer series of documents at the Public Record Office, Chancery Lane, London [9], which has produced one of its explanatory leaflets - number 46 - on Militia Muster Lists and Rolls 1522-1640. Holdings, by counties, for these and subsequent muster and militia lists are detailed in 'Tudor and Stuart Muster Rolls', produced by Alan Dell and Jeremy Gibson; this booklet was first published in 1989 by the Federation of Family History Societies. Detailed commentaries on the militia from 1558 were published by Routledge and Kegan Paul in 1965 and 1967 [10]. Lists for 1535 and 1536, for 1539 and 1540, for 1542 and for 1569 survive for many counties, either at the Public Record Office, the British Library, the Bodleian Library or county record offices, as detailed by Dell and Gibson.

In 1524 and 1525 lay subsidies, further to those of the late fourteenth century, were imposed on a national basis and on top of the previous one tenth and one fifteenth taxes (the so-called Saladin Tithe or Moveables Tax, first imposed in 1181). During the period 1524-25 the methods of taxation were based on three alternative assessments of the taxpayers' capacity : the capital value of property, landed income, and wages. The value of these particular lay subsidies was emphasised by Dr Maurice Beresford [11] who stated "The assessment rolls, where they survive, provide a directory of the upper, middle and lower-middle classes and are near enough to earliest parish registers

(1538) to serve as some basis for genealogical tree planting''.

A list of families in the archdeaconry of Stafford was compiled in 1532. Although not a complete census in that not all inhabitants were listed, it provides some fifty-one thousand names arranged in family groups and states the surname of the head of the family, his Christian name, and the names of his wife and children. The list is unusual because former (deceased) wives and dead children are also included. Its original purpose is uncertain, but it was possibly a list of those entitled to prayers in return for some contribution to church fabric maintenance. As this listing also pertains to the pre-parish register era, its value to British family history for the Stafford locality is immense. An edited and indexed transcription was published in 1976 [12] by the Staffordshire Record Society.

Information on the population of Wales from 1536 to 1801 (or to be more accurate, the paucity of such information) was discussed in 1937 by David Williams in the Bulletin of the Board of Celtic Studies [13], published in Cardiff by the Press Board of the University of Wales.

In 1545 a listing of the population of Kidlington in Oxfordshire was made, thus providing some useful information, particularly as the parish registers there do not commence until 1574. 1545 was an eventful year for Kidlington for in that year the Duke of Suffolk died so that the Manor passed into private hands (those of John Blundell and Leonard Chamberlayne); Henry Lawrence also died, bequeathing his books to Exeter College, Oxford - he was the last Catholic vicar for the parish remaining from prior to the King's break with Rome.

The fascinating Sheep Tax, introduced in March 1549, was debated in some detail by Beresford in the first and second issues of the Agricultural History Review [14] which began as a regular publication of the British Agricultural Historical Society in 1953. The national requirement to tax all flocks of sheep and accordingly to list their size and owners by counties appears to have failed and the 'relief', as it was termed, was discontinued in January 1550. Nevertheless the returns for Huntingdonshire, now in the Public Record Office in Chancery Lane, are very good and those for Yorkshire, listed by Ridings, merit study as do those for Devon, and the counties of Nottingham and Oxford. In a number of cases the names and addresses of flock owners living out of the county (possibly the first example of ''strays'') are given. Such information is valuable in the preparation of a rural social or family history.

On the Statute Books, also for 1549, there is mention of a national Cloth Tax as another means of raising revenue. However, the returns for this "relief" do not appear to have survived and it is uncertain if it was ever enforced or even imposed.

Freemen's Rolls or Registers have already been mentioned (see 1272), and for the City of York another series began in 1559. These, which continued until 1759 in a second volume, were also transcribed, edited by Dr Francis Collins and published [15] by the Surtees Society. Similar listings were made for many other corporate towns.

The 1563 Ecclesiastical Return of Families, which laid down the number of families in every diocese in England, may prove of some value to the family historian; with a suitable multiplier (4.25 is the accepted figure for this return) one can compute the total population for a particular area. Thus a family can be set in the local or the national population context even though the names of individuals are not quoted in the returns. The originals of this return, conducted diocese by diocese, are held among the Harleian Manuscripts [16] in the British Museum.

A schedule of the inhabitants of some Canterbury parishes was compiled around 1565. This contains not only the names of the householders, their wives and the numbers of their children (and in some instances also their names and ages), but also the numbers of their servants. Furthermore, this census must be unique as it also contains the numbers of dogs and hogs kept by each householder. This schedule is deposited at the Kent County Archives Office in Maidstone[17].

The Communicants Lists for Canterbury Diocese in 1565, also deposited at Maidstone [17], are very descriptive for some parishes, especially Eythorne and Waldershare, and amount to almost complete censuses.

A census conducted in Norwich in 1570 was unusual in that it portrayed a relatively large number of people at the bottom of the social ladder. For this reason is sometimes referred to as the "Poor Census". The listing contains names of individuals, their ages, addresses and occupations and in some cases the parishes of their long-time residences or births. It also includes those who were contributing towards the poor rate and identifies master craftsmen and others who had undertaken an apprenticeship but who had temporarily failed; this is apparent as a number of these individuals later apprenticed their sons to other craftsmen. The original census is held at the Norfolk Record Office although an annotated transcription with a descriptive commentary was edited by John F Pound and published by the Norfolk Record Society [18] in 1971.

On 27 May 1571 a certificate portraying the names of all strangers resident and abiding within the port and town of Sandwich, Kent was deposited with the State Papers, held now at the Public Record Office. This listing [19] identifies how many of the strangers were denizens and what was the nation of their origin.

On 5 May 1574 a survey was conducted in Poole, Dorset, by Robert Nicholas and Denis Howse, who were constables of the town. In general each house-holder only is named and there is mention of "his wife" and the numbers of his sons, daughters and servants, although some servants' names are given. Ages or addresses are not generally stated, although those living in the almshouses in two named streets are identified. Also in the census, but taken on 16 July that year, is a list of ships and ship-owners, obviously in Poole harbour, which gives the names of the master and the seafaring men, as well as the name of each vessel and her owner. Included in this census is a note of the names that are to attend and serve at the Castle of Brownsea. The original survey is with the borough archives at Poole, but photocopies are available in Dorset Record Office and Poole Reference Library.

Initiated by a Statute of 1581 and by later statutes, lists were compiled on a national basis from 1582 to 1682, at irregular intervals, of those who absented themselves from divine service at the (Established) parish church. These recusants lists or rolls, now held in the Public Record Office [20], are the annual returns to the Exchequer of the fines and forfeitures imposed; thus they do not contain the names of all the recusants of that time, only those who were compelled to pay. In many cases the recusant's religious denomi-nation is stated. Some of the lists of recusants appear to have been copied contemporarily, probably for the benefit of the diocesan authorities; such copies have found their way into a variety of archives, some now being at the British Museum, some at the House of Lords Record Office, some at the Bodleian Library in Oxford and some are in county record offices. Several of the lists have been transcribed, a selection of which has been published by the Catholic Record Society [21].

At Courteenhall in Northamptonshire, in about 1587, the rector made a list of the parish inhabitants by families with the dates of their births or baptisms. The earliest date on the document is 31 December 1538. The list was added to over subsequent years and developed into a series of pedigree charts, the last addition being made on 28 January 1617. The document was at some later date bound into the first parish register for Courteenhall, and is now in the county archives [22] in Northampton.

1590 is an example of a year that might have become the genealogists' fulcrum, not because of a census as such but the potential for everybody's name being recorded on a national basis. Lord Burghley, Lord Treasurer at the time, sent a proposal to the Archbishop of Canterbury for the establishment of a General Register Office. Unfortunately over 200 years had to pass before such a proposal fell on sympathetic ears.

The original of the Caernarvonshire Subsidy Roll for 1597/8 is typical of a census in this form which has been deposited in the Public Record Office [23]. The list of names was transcribed, edited and published in 1937 with a commentary by Emyr Gwynne Jones in the Bulletin of the Board of Celtic Studies [24].

In 1599 Richard Phillips (constable) and William Gurnall (headborough) conducted a census of Ealing, Middlesex and included the names, occupations and ages of the inhabitants. The original material is held in the Public Record Office [25] but a transcript was published by Ealing Local History Society in 1962. This provides a most valuable list at the end of the sixteenth century of the inhabitants of a Middlesex village now swallowed up as a suburb of Greater London.

3. Seventeenth century listings

Two censuses were conducted in the borough of Marlborough Wiltshire, in 1600 and 1601. The first, in June 1600 is a list of those in the borough who contributed financially towards the purchase of armour or armoury for the fight against Spain. It was accordingly known locally as a levy towards "Armour for the Armada". The 1601 census was conducted to ascertain the names of those men in the borough who were between the ages of 17 and 60, and was thus a militia muster listing (see 1522) rather than a true census. Men in this age range were considered capable of bearings arms, and so fit to fight, presumably against the Spaniards; taking this and the subscription raised the previous year into account there must have been some considerable anti-Iberian feeling in Marlborough, at least, at this period.

Manorial surveys were conducted in many parts of the country from around the year 1600. The ownerships of tenements were traced back to their owner "ex antiquo", which in practice amounted from about sixty to seventy years. Such surveys provide surnames retaining the same tenements and thus a history of the tenancies. For example at Barton-le-Cley, Bedfordshire, a house with eighteen acres which was occupied by John Foster in 1603 was previously occupied by Thomas Rudd, who had taken it over from John Rudd, who had taken it over from Richard Ellis in 1551, who had taken it over from a Mr Burnard in 1512. It is interesting to note in this case that by 1671 only the Foster surname was still extant in the parish. The decline (or increase) in the fortunes of a family can also be traced through a study of these surveys by noting the amounts paid, or even exemptions permitted, for successive years.

Another national enumeration for ecclesiastical purposes, similar to the 1563 census, was made in 1603, but this time the numbers of communicants in each parish were noted. Some of these communicants lists are in the British Museum [26], some in county record offices, and others in diocesan record offices (mostly given to the care of the county archivist today). Many of the

1603 lists have been transcribed and published [27].

In 1608 a census was taken of men in Gloucestershire. This described their occupations and indicated the distribution of industries in the county. The original return is in the county archives but an analysis and commentary [28] on the census was published in the Economic History Review in 1934.

The total population of Guernsey in 1615 has been estimated in several histories of the island, such as found in Ansted and Latham's work on the Channel Islands in 1862. A commentary by G H Dury on the Guernsey figures was published [29] in the quarterly journal of the Geographical Association in 1948.

At irregular intervals between 1618 and 1628 detailed lists of the inhabitants of the village of Cogenhoe, Northamptonshire, were compiled by Christopher Spicer, the rector, and included in his parish registers. In some years he listed the individuals alphabetically by Christian names, in other years alphabetically by family surname, and other years apparently arbitrarily. For those who have ancestors in that tiny community these lists would prove a fascinating study even though it is by no means a true census. The parish register containing the original surveys is in the county record office in Northampton.

In 1622 a census was undertaken of the inhabitants of the borough of Stafford. A commentary on this census was written by Ruth M Kidson and published in the Transactions of the Old Stafford Society for 1956-59. The original returns [30] are in the County Record Office at Stafford.

A list of the Vills and Freeholders of Derbyshire was made in 1633, although the original purpose of the list is uncertain. What appeared to be a draft manuscript of this listing was held privately (by G A Cubley of Sheffield) in 1884. Fortunately, however, it was transcribed by Sidney Oldall Addy who published the names of the vills and the individual freeholders in the annual volume [31] of the Derbyshire Archaeological and Natural History Society for that year.

A survey of the inhabitants of the City of London was undertaken in 1638 as a result of an order of the King in Council dated 22 April 1638. The clergy of London were required to make an estimate of the rental value of the houses in each of the 107 City parishes together with the actual tithe paid for each house. The original returns, which are now in Lambeth Palace Library, for

93 of the City parishes contain the names of householders, the rentals paid for the houses and the tithes paid. Some incumbents described the locations of the houses in their parishes in great detail, others did not even state the Christian names of the householders; thus the information for each parish varies enormously. Nevertheless an edited, but usefully indexed, transcription of this return was published in 1931 by the Society of Genealogists.

Another list of the City of London, but this time of the "Principal Inhabitants" was made in 1640, by wards. The returns, held in the Public Record Office, list the inhabitants in each ward who were prepared to assist Charles I by offering financial security; the wards were arranged alphabetically, but there are no inhabitants for some wards on the list. A copy of the list was made and published in 1886 "from original returns in the Public Record Office made by the Aldermen of the several wards of the City of London, naming such Inhabitants as were conceived able to lend the King (Charles I) money upon security raising £200,000, according to order of the Privy Council, dated 10 May 1640". The list was republished more usefully by Pinhorns in 1969 who added an index of the names compiled by C F H Evans.

On 30 July 1641, with the prospect of civil war looming over the English horizon, the House of Commons asked all males over the age of eighteen to maintain "the true Reformed Protestant Religion", "His Majestie's Royal Person" and "the Privileges of Parliament" among other oaths. Conducted on a national basis these Protestation Returns [32], now kept in the House of Lords Record Office, are particularly useful in determining on which side an ancestor stood at this period in history. The returns list not only those who agreed, and thus signed or made their mark, but also those who refused to sign. For some counties every return has survived and in many cases transcripts have been made and published in recent years; however, for other counties all are lost.

For 1651 another estimate of the population of Guernsey (see 1615) has been made and similarly commented upon.

From the mid-seventeenth century many further taxes were imposed and the consequent lists of the taxpayers are most useful sources of names. The sums which were paid in many cases indicate the financial worth of either the individuals concerned or the property which they occupied or owned - in any case such information is invaluable in the compilation of a family history.

The range of taxes include poll tax listings from 1660 to 1700 which had their origins in similar taxes imposed from 1222. These poll tax lists contain the names of adults and children over 16 years of age, although sometimes only the numbers of children, not their names, are stated. The originals of many of these lists have found their way into county record offices, although the Public Record Office also holds a considerable number.

The names of those who in 1661 contributed towards a ''free and voluntary gift'' on a county by county basis appear on the lists that were compiled in that year. It is believed that public collections were made on market days. The original lists have been deposited in county record offices. The ''gift'' was to celebrate the return of Charles II to the throne, and so the names of the donors are likely to be only those who supported the restoration of the monarchy, or those who believed it expedient to display their names on such lists. Original documents for over thirty counties are known to be extant.

In 1662, and annually until 1688, the ancient Saxon Fumage Tax, based on the number of chimneys at a dwelling, was revived as a Hearth Tax; but this time the tax was payable in two instalments, on Lady Day and on Michaelmas Day, on the number of firehearths or fireplaces, unless the occupier was exempt by reason of poverty. Strictly, there were two lists generated on each occasion, the assessment of the amount payable, and the return which carried the amount actually paid. The surviving documents do not readily distinguish one from the other and all are generally referred to as returns. Those for 1662 listed only the taxable hearths but after 1663 all hearths were itemised. The original lists have been deposited in the relevant county record offices and are usually catalogued among the Quarter Sessions material. However, duplicate copies were made centrally by the Exchequer clerks in London and these duplicates, which are deposited in the Public Record Office at Chancery Lane are considerably easier to read. JSWG has provided a county by county directory [33] of the location of Hearth Tax assessments and returns. The Hearth Tax returns for 1664, which were compiled on Lady Day, are the most complete. This tax, which was levied at two shillings per fireplace, should have raised £1,200,000 per year but there was considerable opposition and much evasion, and even resulted in riots in Bristol and London. In the event some years realised a mere £170,000 and at the most only £700,000 a year was raised. Few officials bothered to collect the tax after 1674 and it was formally abolished in 1688. But the lists do contain names of individuals with the number of fireplaces on which they were taxed (or from which they were exempt). The numbers of hearths have been used by statisticians to calculate the populations of communities at this period, the usual multiplier being 4.5 times the number of listed hearths.

In 1665 Bills of Mortality were instituted to provide data on deaths due to the plague. These continued, in some areas on an annual basis, long after 1665 and provide colourful descriptions of causes of death in the seventeenth and even later centuries. The data, however, was derived not very carefully, in many cases from parish registers, and no allowance appears to have been made of non-conformists failing to register most baptisms and some burials. Thus the data is not always very accurate even though the Bills do make fascinating reading.

At Coleridge, Devon in 1670 a subscription was raised for Turkish prisoners of war. Those who contributed were listed by name, so providing an indica- tion of those with some means in the parish, or at least those with some sympathy towards the prisoners. The original subscription list has been deposited in the Devon record office in Plymouth.

On 8 October 1673 the inhabitants within the manor and parish of Swindon, Wiltshire were listed. The names of the juries and homage that served in the court that year were also specifically mentioned. The list may now be consulted in Swindon reference library.

The most widely documented census of 1676 is the Compton or Sheldon enumeration. Compton, who was a Bishop of London living from 1632 to 1713 collected some comprehensive statistics on families living in England and Wales on behalf of Gilbert Sheldon who was Archbishop of Canterbury from 1663 to 1677. Hence either name is applied to this parish-by-parish listing which is mainly numbers of conformists, papists and nonconformists. However, not a few returns name the dissenters whilst other returns name all the inhabitants of particular parishes. Some original returns are in the Can- terbury Cathedral Archives [34] , others are in Lambeth Palace [35] and there is an eighteenth century copy of the returns for the Province of Canterbury in the William Salt Library [36], Stafford. The background history to this census was discussed in detail by Dr Thomas Richards, recently appointed Librarian of University College, Bangor, in a supplement [37] to the annual publication of the Honourable Society of Cymmrodorion for 1927; whilst the greater part of that article made particular reference to Welsh archdeaconries and parishes, the first fifteen or so pages explain the generic origins of this enumeration. An article [38] by E A Whiteman in 1986 provided an even more comprehensive account. Some of the returns and surveys resulting from Compton's census are described below.

An analysis of the results for the Dioceses of Canterbury and Rochester was made by Christopher William Chalkin and made available by the Records Publication Committee of the Kent Archaeological Society [39] in 1960.

The listing of the names of the inhabitants of Wrotham and Stansted, Kent, is an example conducted in Shoreham Deanery in 1676. A commentary on this census was also published by the Kent Archaeological Society [40].

On 7 April 1676, Francis Nicholson the curate-in-charge at Goodnestone-next-Wingham, Kent, commenced an account of his parishioners, according to their "families, quality and religion". Nicholson used the term "quality" to distinguish between gentlemen, yeomen, tradesmen, labourers and poor men. This most useful listing of named inhabitants was probably prompted by Bishop Compton's request. Nicholson's original account is deposited in the Canterbury Cathedral Library.

A similar listing of parishes and the number of communicants, together with the numbers of catholics, quakers and dissenters was prepared in 1676 for the Diocese of Carlisle. A commentary on this was published by Francis Godwin James [41] in 1952 with an additional comment on the apparent discrepancy between the numbers of "persons of age to communicate" and of those confirmed. The returns for Lincolnshire were transcribed by Arthur S Langley and published in Lincolnshire Notes and Queries [42] in 1920, those for Nottinghamshire were published [43] in 1924 by the Thoroton Society, while those for Suffolk appeared in that county's Local History Council publication, Suffolk Review [44] in 1966. A reference to the Peterborough Diocesan returns, where the headings appear as numbers of "Familyes, Prns young and old, Popish Recusants and Obstinate separatists" was published in Local Population Studies [45] in 1973, although the figures for only six parishes were transcribed.

At Clayworth, Nottinghamshire, the rector, William Sampson, conducted his own census of his parish in 1676 and again 1688, providing what appear to be comprehensive lists of the inhabitants. The 1676 census was more than likely prompted by Compton's request as Sampson took his survey on 9 April; but it appears to have begun life as a subscription list on behalf of the inhabitants of Northampton who were suffering from the devastating effects of a fire which had swept through that town. Both the 1676 and the 1688 censuses of Clayworth, but especially the former, have been the subjects of extensive studies by population scholars [46] who have compared them with other local lists and drawn numerous conclusions. Abstracts from the 1676 list are, therefore, quoted in many articles, although a complete copy of the original may be found in the Nottinghamshire Record Office [47].

1677 saw the publication by Samuel Lee of 'A Collection of the Names of the Merchants Living In and About the City of London'. Although by no means a real census this publication was the first English directory and does provide names, occupations and addresses. Over successive years trade and private directories were published for counties, cities, towns and villages throughout the British Isles. Whilst such directories are beyond the scope of this cameo, their "census like" content should not be overlooked. Descriptive accounts including the publications of Sketchley, White, Bains, Hunt, Pigot and Kelly with their historical background to 1856 were related in 1932 by Charles WF Goss [48] for the London area, and in 1950 and 1984 by Jane E Norton [49] for the remainder of England and Wales.

Lists of Papists were again made in 1680, those lists now being kept at the House of Lords Record Office [50]. The Eleventh Report of the Historical Manuscripts Commission in describing this holding indicates the number of papists in each county (Northamptonshire had 8 whilst Monmouthshire had 189), but for some counties (eg Herefordshire) the names of individuals are given in the abstract.

In 1684 lists were made by ministers in seventeen parishes in Wigtownshire and Minnigaff in Scotland of all the inhabitants over the age of 12. The purpose was probably to gather information on the potential military strength in the area relating to the Covenanters, the more extreme of whom were strongly opposed to the restored monarch, Charles II, in his attitude towards the Solemn League and Covenant. For some of the seventeen parishes, relationships between individuals were noted. A transcription of these lists was edited by William Scott and published by the Scottish Record Society

[51] in 1916.

Also in 1684 a census including the names and ages of individuals was held at Chilvers Coton in Warwickshire. The original returns are in the record office in Warwick.

Additionally in 1684 a valuation was conducted in the parishes of Box, Ditchridge and Haslebury, Wiltshire. Names of adult males were included in the lists made at the time, thus providing a pseudo-census for those parishes. The original valuation is deposited in the Wiltshire Record Office in Trowbridge.

Abstracts from surveys of London, taken for various purposes in 1687 and 1690 were quoted by Dr Richard Price [52] in his 'Observations on Reversionary Payments' in its various editions from 1771 to 1812. The number of houses, but not families, in London in 1687 calculated from Hearth Tax Returns (qv) was first referred to by Sir William Petty in 'Political Arithmetic' (pp 74 and 79); in Dr Davenant's Works (Vol 1 p 38) the 1690 figures for London (and all other counties) were analysed. Price became deeply involved in writing and presenting papers, particularly to the Royal Society, on various aspects of population figures. He not only drew on surveys, such as those for London of the seventeenth century, but he encouraged many colleagues in the eighteenth century to personally undertake other surveys and supply him with their results. Many such surveys, enumerations and censuses used by Price in his theses are referred to below.

In 1691 a survey was undertaken in Adel, near to Leeds. It was mentioned in 1948 [53] as "being in a commonplace book belonging to John Lucas in Leeds Public Library".

A Parliamentary Act for the registration of births, marriages and burials became effective from 1 May 1695 for a period of five years. The purpose was to tax each registration in order to raise revenue "for carrying on the war with France with Vigour" in which England was indulging at that time. The tax was complicated in that it was graduated according to status, and the Act was complicated in that it required births to be registered within five days and the events to be recorded on certificates for each Parish, Division, Constablewick, Allotment and Place; but the Act did not state what should be written on the certificates, although it did state that they should be forwarded to the Commissioners of the Act for the first year (as for the Land Tax) and to the county Justices for the remaining four years. Unfortunately the Act also failed to state what should happen to the certificates thereafter, which may explain the random survival of the returns of what is often called the Marriage Duty Act. The Act was further convoluted in attempting to extract duties from bachelors and widowers, and requiring detailed statistics on nobility and gentry For a full description of this Act see the Chapmans Records Cameo 'Marriage Laws, Rites and Customs'.

In spite of all the confusion many assessors did produce annual returns, and included the name, estate, degree, and title of each individual and how much tax was payable. Servants, women and children were also included; thus these returns, where they have survived, form excellent censuses. Unfortunately no centrally-maintained lists appear to have been kept, presumably because of the confusion as to what to do with the certificates once collected, and there are no complete lists for every county. In fact for many counties most lists have been lost, but where they do survive they offer very useful data, actually over a longer period than originally intended as the Act was not repealed until 1705, rather than the planned date of 1700. For Lyme Regis, Dorset, lists were made in 1695, 1697, 1699, 1701, 1702 and 1703 which are now in the county record office. The 1695 listing for London is one of the most useful; the original return is in the Corporation of London Record Office [54], the staff of which indexed the return in 1966 under surnames, places and trades. The 1698 listing for Fenny Compton, taken on 7 April, disappeared into private hands until 1883 when a descendant of one of the 1698 church-wardens presented the original to the rector, who kept it with the parish records; a commentary on the list (but not a transcription) was made by Philip Styles [55] in 1951, drawing comparisons with other lists. There is a similar listing for Bristol and another for the thirty-six townships in the Wingham Petty Division of Kent, although the latter was taken during the last year that the Act was in force - 1705. The original returns for the Wingham Division have been deposited in the Kent County Archives.

A list of the inhabitants of Melbourne, Derbyshire with their "title and qualifications" (actually their trades and occupations) was made in 1695, as a consequence of the Marriage Duty Act quoted above. The list states the required information, ie the amounts of duty paid for burials, marriages, births, bachelors and widows, but also indicates a few individuals aged 25.

During the last century the Melbourne list was discussed in an article [56] published in the Journal of the Derbyshire Archaeological and Natural History Society. At that time the list was held privately by Viscount Hardinge, it having been passed down in his family from an ancestor who was one of the Justices of the Peace who signed and allowed the original assessment in 1695. Unfortunately its present whereabouts are unknown, thus illustrating the value of transcripts and copies of original documents, and the necessity for them to be deposited in secure archives. A similar list for Donhead, Wiltshire has been discovered among the parish chest material, whilst one for New Romney, Kent was in the town records.

Also in 1695 all public office holders were required by an Act of Parliament to take an oath of loyalty or Association to William and Mary and an oath that should these monarchs be assassinated by Jacobite supporters they would take revenge on them. Thus Association Oath Rolls, which contain the signatures of the loyal officers, were compiled on a county basis, in some cases subdivided into hundreds and boroughs. But these rolls were made available for any citizens of England and Wales and English colonies overseas to sign; therefore, the lists, which are now at the Public Record Office in Chancery Lane, London, contain many adult males and in some cases female householders as well, such that for some areas almost complete censuses of the adult population were created. The clergy signed separate rolls which were collected and collated by deanery and diocese and these are filed this way today. A catalogue of the extant Association Oath Rolls was prepared by Clifford Webb [57] in 1983.

Gregory King, known to many as the "Father of Population Studies", began his study on the 'Natural and Political Observations upon the State and Condition of England' in 1695. Although he had completed this by the following year his observations were not published until 1802 when they appeared as an appendix to George Chambers' work 'An Estimate of the Comparative Strength of Great Britain'. King was not only Lancaster Herald but also a draughtsman, heraldic painter, engraver, cartographer, surveyor and architect. As a herald he would have conducted heraldic visitations and it is believed that he used the same material to calculate the population - although it is not known how. It is also possible that he took the number of houses quoted in the Hearth Tax returns (qv) and used a suitable multiplier to arrive at a population figure. It is more probable that he used data from the

1694 Taxation Act returns together with his own surveys to derive the numbers for the population. A variety of commentaries on King's work have been published over the years [58].

In Scotland, a poll tax was imposed during 1695 by the Scottish Parliament to augment existing revenue sources; this was in order to increase the efficiency of the army and navy to combat danger from foreign and internal (including English) enemies. An earlier poll tax imposed in 1693 had been a failure. The returns for Aberdeenshire and Renfrewshire and a few scattered parishes in Scotland are in the record office in Edinburgh; those for the former county were published in two volumes in 1844 as a 'List of Pollable Persons within the Shire of Aberdeen'. The information to be found in the returns is useful as they state the name, status, place of residence and occupation of every person who was over 16 and not a pauper (a burden on the parish). A commentary [59] on the returns by Kenneth Walton was published in 1950.

In Dublin an exact survey of the number of inhabitants was undertaken, together with surveys for the counties of Armagh, Lowth and Meath; the results of these were communicated by Captain South to the Royal Society, published in their 'Philosophical Transactions' and also quoted by Price [60], as was a similar survey of Maidstone, Kent.

In 1696 a Window Tax was introduced and remained in force (with some modifications made during the reign of George III) until replaced in 1851 by a House Duty Tax which was abolished in 1924. The Window Tax, granted to William III, was introduced initially to generate sufficient income to enable the Royal Mint to make up the deficiency caused by individuals feloniously clipping fragments off silver coins to collect and sell the silver. The tax paid for the reminting of the damaged coins and also retrieved for the treasury the value of the lost silver. The records of this tax, for which there was a separate return for each township, contain the name and address of each taxpayer, the number of windows on which tax was paid and the money collected. Hospitals, charity schools, almshouses and workhouses were also assessed as if the tax was to be applied but they were each granted an exemption certificate, as were churches and chapels. Dairies and cheese-rooms were also exempt from tax so long as their windows were unglazed and their outer doors and the outside of their windows were clearly identified with large painted letters stating "Dairy" or "Cheese Room". Large windows were assessed as two. The Royal Family was also exempt from paying. Similarly to the Hearth Tax, the Window Tax offers an indication of the social status of an ancestor, as well as his abode, even though the tax was in general badly administered and many of the returns have been lost by today. Window Tax returns, whilst not prolific for most areas of the country, may be located in county record offices, in many cases filed with the Quarter Sessions records.

In the Bedfordshire village of Pavenham a census was taken in 1699; the names of the villagers and in some cases their occupations were recorded in the parish register. This is now deposited in the county record office in Bedford.

4. Eighteenth century listings - the first half

Enumerations of the inhabitants of Liverpool appear to have been taken every decade from 1700 until 1770 at least, as the figures were quoted in 1773 by Dr W Enfield in the second edition of 'An Essay towards the history of Leverpool'. Enfield was a 'lecturer on the Belles Lettres in the Academy at Warrington' and may have influenced the undertaking of a survey there as well when his book was published (see 1773 below when yet another enumeration for Liverpool was undertaken). Dr J Aikin also commented on the population of Liverpool during the eighteenth century in his book on Manchester (page 335 et seq) published in 1795 (see 1781 below).

A census was undertaken of communicants within the ancient parish of Stoke-upon-Trent in 1701. Four years later Samuel Paulson, the parish clerk, copied the details which are now in the Staffordshire Record Office [61]. The copy, which unfortunately appears to be of only part of the total parish, lists the names and ages of the communicants by household; the head is named first followed by his wife, the children and the servants. Widows, single women, and adult brothers and sisters who acted as joint heads of households are also identified.

A population survey of Minehead, Somerset, which was undertaken in 1705 is referred to by John Collinson, the vicar of Long Ashton, [62] in his 'History and Antiquities of the County of Somerset....', published in 1791. The number of houses and their location were included in this survey although the whereabouts of the original are not now known.

In 1705 Deputy Lieutenants were required, by an Order in Council of 18 January 1705, to supply statistics on Papists. For some counties, Cheshire, for example, names were compiled into lists which are now among the House of Lords records; however, for most counties no papists were located and a typical response [63], such as that from Anglesey, stated "we are so happy in this county that we have never a Papist but one, and he is a person of mean fortune and an old man ....'''. Shortly afterwards, on 2 March 1705, apparently as a result of the poor response to the first request, the House of Lords asked archbishops and bishops to supply the same statistics; on this occasion the responses were more fruitful, although not all bishops appear to have reacted positively. Those who did often provided names of the Papists, and for the Diocese of London occupations were also given; the latter lists are in the Guildhall Library [64]. Others, such as those for the Diocese of Chester which state names and occupations, may be consulted in the House of Lords Record Office [65].

The regular Visitations of the Archbishops throughout the eighteenth century in many instances contain numbers of Papists in each parish. In a few of these Visitations names of the Papists appear. A number of the returns compiled by the ecclesiastical clerks have been transcribed by bodies such as the Catholic Record Society; more locally interested groups, the Yorkshire Archaeological Society for example, have published the returns for their particular area. The Church Commissioners retain, among the Fulham Palace Papers, the responses to queries sent to London and Westminster parishes in 1765 [66].

The potential growth in Roman Catholicism was of such concern to some clerics that on 4 August 1706 the Archbishop of Canterbury was persuaded to secure an Order in Council requiring every incumbent to take an exact account of the number of Papists and reputed Papists in his parish; the incumbent was further required to state the papists' qualities, estates and places of abode. This Order also enquired what advowsons or rights of presentation or donation of churches, benefices or schools were in the disposition of Papists or reputed papists. The House of Lords Record Office holds the diocesan summaries for many dioceses, although there are some locally held lists in county record offices [67]. The majority of these lists and summaries have been transcribed and many have been published by the Catholic Record Society [68].

Between 1706 and 1721 surveys for the Diocese of Lincoln were produced by the incumbents or archdeacons between 1706 and 1721, obviously in response to the 1706 Order in Council. That taken by the Church authorities at Boston, Lincolnshire in 1709 may well be an example of the Papist survey request. However, in the case of Boston, neither the original returns nor any analysis appear to have survived although the survey itself, and the total figure of the population are mentioned in Thompson's 'History of Boston', published in 1856.

The numbers of families in each of the Cheshire parishes of Oldham, Chaderton, Royton and Crompton in 1714, and comparisons with the numbers in 1789 and 1792 were made by Dr J Aikin in 1795 in his book (p 242) on Manchester (see 1781 below).

Register Rolls of Papists were kept by the Ely diocesan authorities from 1716 to 1744, and as such have remained among the bishops' records; in most cases where they survive, these are now in the pertinent county record offices. A similar series from 1723-48 for the Diocese of London is in the Guildhall Library [69]. Numbers of people on the Hertfordshire lists were most competently discussed in 1964 [70] by Lionel Munby, together with many other figures available in a variety of ecclesiastical sources, in one of the publications of that county's Local History Council.

In 1723 many individuals swore an Oath of Allegiance before their county justices "pursuant to the late act 9 Georgii Regis", thus providing not only a list of names of potential ancestors and their "places of aboad", but also their declared loyalty to the crown. For most counties the lists have been filed with the Quarter Sessions material in the county archives; for Cheshire, four small volumes of these lists survive among the sessions records, whereas at York there is a list of 1800 inhabitants, with occupations, in the City Council Minute Book.

At Puddleton, Dorset a census was taken of the parishioners in 1724-25 by the vicar. The originals of this return are now deposited in the county record office at Dorchester.

In 1727 Guernsey was again (see 1615 and 1651) the subject of an estimate of the population figures. This, like those of the earlier estimates, was quoted by Dury in his article referred to above.

An enumeration was undertaken in each parish at Cambridge in 1728, probably by Bowtell in preparation for his 'History of Cambridge'. The work, which was intended to comprise several volumes, was never published but his draft notes [71] were deposited with his other manuscripts in the library of Downing College, Cambridge. The total population figure of 6422 in

Bowtell's work was quoted by Charles Henry Cooper, who also rearranged the parish lists into alphabetical order, in his 'Annals of Cambridge', published in 1852 [72].

In 1730, for Douglas, Isle of Man, a list was drawn up of the names of residents ("housekeepers" is the term used in the original document although in many cases an apparent husband and wife are both named as the housekeeper); the numbers of their children, servants, and lodgers and strangers were also given. This list, edited with some introductory notes by William Harrison, was printed in 1878 but published [73] in 1880 as the second volume of Manx Miscellanies by the Manx Society. The published list has some 35 fewer households than the original, now in the Douglas archives. Within the introductory notes is reference to an account of the number of souls in Douglas from a paper of Bishop Wilson in 1726 and also to a similar return by the Clergy in 1757; the latter itemises numbers of married couples, widowers, widows, adult single men, adult single women, males under 16 and females under 16. There is also reference to the same breakdown of population made on 29 January 1784 by Thomas W J Woods, Vicar of Braddan, by order of Edward Smith, the Governor. The Commissioners Report for 1792, Appendix B Nos 89, 90, & 91 quoted the figures. It may be noted here that the taking of a census every ten years did not begin on the island until 1811, in contrast to 1801 for England and Wales.

The registers of Papists requested by the House of Lords for the diocesan authorities have already been referred to. In some cases, though, they are mixed with the returns made in preparation for the ecclesiastical visitations. Those of 1735 sent to Archbishop Blackburn for the diocese of York are a good example; a transcript of these was published by the Catholic Record Society in 1907 [74], and the returns for York city and part of Ainsty were published, with comment, in the 'Northern Genealogist' in 1900.

In 1736, by order of the Town Burgesses, an enumeration was made at Sheffield to ascertain the population of the city prior to a petition being presented in Parliament to make St Paul's Church parochial. The number of families and individuals in the township of Sheffield, in Brightside, Dyerlow, Attercliffe-cum-Darnall, Ecclesall and the two Hallams was recorded. In his 'Hallamshire', Joseph Hunter [75] has quoted figures from a manuscript of Dr Thomas Short regarding this enumeration.

On Jersey, on 10 June 1737, an enumeration was conducted of the numbers of houses and inhabitants in each parish. The numbers of men, women and children under 14 and those at sea "en service" and "à Terreneuve" were identified separately. The original document, which is in the University Library, Cambridge [76] , has only ten of the twelve parishes, even though its title clearly states "chaque paroisse" (each parish). For seven of the ten parishes the statistics are subdivided into vingtaines. No names are included in the parish enumerations which total 13,642 persons. There is a copy of the original in the Library of the Channel Islands Family History Society.

In 1737 Dr William Maitland [77] made an estimate "with incredible pains" "from the parish books" of the number of houses in London. Similar estimates and attempts to distinguish cottages from houses were made in subsequent years (1758, 1761, 1765, 1777, for example) from the returns of the window tax surveyors. Papers on these figures were read at meetings of the Royal Society and published in their Philosophical Transactions in 1756, 1758 and 1760. Price further referred to this data in his 'Observations'; although Maitland had originally published his figures (together with others for 1627 to 1635 and for 1728 to 1737) in 1739 in his own 'History of London from its foundation by the Romans to the present time....with the several accounts of Westminster, Middlesex, Southwark and other parts within the Bill of Mortality'.

An account of the number of inhabitants of Chelmsford, Essex in 1738 was mentioned by Philip Morant in his 'History and Antiquities of the County of Essex....', published in 1768 [78]. Morant quotes only the total population and the original survey does not appear to be extant.

An enumeration of 1739 for Nottingham was described by George Charles Deering in his 'Nottinghamia vetus et nova, or an historical account of the ancient and present state of....Nottingham....' in 1751. Whilst Deering refers to the numbers of houses and their location, as well as the total population figures, the original returns do not appear to have survived. An index to Deering's work by Rupert Cecil Chicken was published in 1899.

At Aynho in Northamptonshire a list of names of the families and numbers of persons was made on 30 December 1740. Against each family on the list the number of servants and the number of family members were identified and the total number of 125 families, 82 servants and 567 persons given at the end of the list. A check was evidently made subsequently as in another hand a further four families were identified and added to the list. On two sheets of otherwise plain paper this list is amongst the parochial documents of Aynho in the Northampton County Archives.

In 1741 the inhabitants of Farnham, Surrey were enumerated. At that time Farnham was a mere village with less than 2000 people - a sharp contrast to the Farnham of the twentieth century. This enumeration was referred to nearly forty years later by William Wales in his 'An Inquiry into the Present State of the Population of England and Wales' published in 1781 (qv). The original document from which Wales quoted appears to be missing.

At Olveston, Gloucestershire 'the number and names of the inhabitants... which do actually live upon the spot [were] taken in the year 1742 by Chris: Shute Vicar'. In fact Rev Cristopher (sic) Shute listed only the names of the 125 heads of the households and indicated "his wife" and the numbers of servants and children in the tythings of Olveston and Tockington. An article on this census with the names, the original of which is in Bristol Record office, Olveston now being in the county of Avon, appeared in the fifteenth quarterly journal of the Bristol and Avon Family History Society in the Spring of 1979.

A survey of the numbers of families and inhabitants including the numbers of males and females was conducted in 1743 for Edinburgh's parish of St Cuthbert. This was referred to in 1753 by William Maitland [79] in his 'History of Edinburgh from its Foundation to the Present Time....' and was further quoted by Price [80].

Population figures for Gloucester in 1743 appear among the Furneys papers [81] in the Bodleian Library. The figures, which included the number of married couples and the number of houses, were published in 1819 by Thomas Dudley Fosbroke in his 'Original History of the City of Gloucester.... including also the original papers of....R Bigland' [82]. The Visitation Returns required by the diocesan authorities are useful for York diocese for 1743; the information sent to Archbishop Herring included details on Papists and has been published by the Yorkshire Archaeological Society [83] in four of its volumes.

A list of the inhabitants of Stanton St Bernard, Wiltshire was made in 1744.

This list is to be found in the Wiltshire Record Office at Trowbridge.

In 1746 an enumeration was conducted in Northampton which included the numbers of houses and inhabitants. For the parishes of All Saints and St Giles the surveys detailed males and females, servants, lodgers and children; for St Peter's parish the numbers were broken down only to males and females and for St Sepulchre's to adults and children. Price subsequently [84] thanked Mr Lawton for obtaining the figures. The results of this survey were the subject of some detailed discussion over a century later in 1847 by William Farr [85] who was then the Registrar General; in his Report for Commissioners, Farr commented on Northampton Life Tables and the results of Bills of Mortality both generally and specifically.

Detail on the population of Hertford was collected in 1747 as it was felt that the existing estimated figures were out of date. A letter to the 'Gentlemen's Magazine' [86] in July of that year advised that the correspondent had undertaken this survey "by particular enquiry" in the ancient town in the parishes of St Andrew, All Saints and St John. The survey distinguished between members of the Established Church, Dissenters and Quakers.

A carriage tax was introduced in 1747 and remained in force until 1782. Carriages with four wheels were taxed at a higher rate than those with two, and two wheeled carriages drawn by two horses incurred a higher duty than than those drawn by one horse. Carts were also taxed unless such carts were used in the affairs of husbandry or carriage of goods in the course of trade, in which case the words "Common Stage Cart" and the name and address of the owner had to be painted on the side of the cart. Whilst not a census, the lists of those who paid this tax do furnish names of individuals and imply their social standing; the vast majority of the population could not afford to own or operate a carriage or cart on which this duty was payable, thus those whose names do appear on the carriage tax lists would have been in the upper stratum of society.

In 1748 a survey was undertaken of the numbers of houses and families in the city and liberties of Edinburgh. Similarly to the 1743 survey (qv) this was referred to by Maitland [87] and Price [88].

Thomas Jeffereys engraved a number of maps between 1748 and 1750, particularly for towns in the Midlands of England. Whilst he utilised information furnished by various surveyors, in many cases Jeffereys included population figures for the towns which he depicted on his maps. For example, the numbers of houses and inhabitants in Coventry (1748) and in Birmingham (1750) were quoted on the maps which he engraved from Bradford's surveys of those two towns. He similarly quoted the numbers of houses and inhabitants on the maps he engraved from Isaac Taylor's surveys in 1750 for Wolverhampton, Staffordshire, in 1751 for Oxford and in 1757 for Hereford.

In 1749 Cambridge was subject to another (see 1728) enumeration, but for this year the numbers of houses, besides the breakdown of the population figures into parishes within the city were identified. The figures were "collected from house to house" and published in Edmund Carter's 'History of the County of Cambridge from the Earliest Account to the Present Time' in 1753 [89]. It would appear that at least one of the original collections "from house to house" has survived; this contains names of householders and numbers in each house for St Benedict's parish, and is in the record office at Cambridge [90]. Two other listings containing names, for the parishes of St Giles and St Peter, which include 'the number of souls in every family, and the religion they profess' are stuck in the back covers of a copy of 'The history and antiquities of Barnwell Abbey and of Sturbridge Fair' which has been deposited in the Bodleian Library Oxford [91]. However, comparing the numbers on these lists with Carter's figures it would appear that these two listings were made around 1760.

5. Eighteenth century listings - 1750 to 1775

On 30 April 1750 a list was compiled of 184 French Protestants "that have left France for their religion and are now residing in the Island of Jersey". The purpose of compiling such a list appears to have been to identify to the English government suitable "foreign Protestants" to send to Nova Scotia as acceptable settlers in that colony. The English who had been sent to Halifax the previous year had not stayed in the town, and the authorities were anxious for the colony to succeed, but not as a Catholic settlement. It would appear, however, that the people listed were not sent to Nova Scotia, and thus put down roots in Jersey. The original of this list, which is in the Colonial Office records [92] of Nova Scotia, contains the names, occupations and ages in years and months of the French Protestants. A transcript was made by Terrence M Punch and published in the Channel Islands Family History Journal [93] in 1988, although there are copies in the Channel Islands Family History Society library and that of La Société Jersiaise, St Helier, Jersey.

A survey was undertaken in 1750 for Shrewsbury, Shropshire by John Leigh who also, similarly to the work undertaken for Northampton in 1746, prepared Bills of Mortality. Leigh, however, included an analysis of the age of the inhabitants of the town as well as the number of houses and their parochial location. The enumeration resulting from the 1750 survey was included in the 1754 Bill for Shrewsbury. For the parish of Holy Cross the numbers of families and inhabitants were further recorded by the vicar, Rev William Gorsuch; he also kept detailed notes of the numbers of males under 10, females under 10, males between 70 and 80, females between 70 and 80, males over 80 and females over 80. Gorsuch repeated his surveys every five years until 1780, making his results available to Price and the Royal Society [94], who published his findings in 1761, 1771 and 1782.

John Browning of Barton Hill, Bristol calculated the number of inhabitants of the City of Bristol in 1751 "from the burials over a period of ten years, and from the number of houses from the 1751 land-tax". He obviously took a great deal of care with his calculations because he "consulted the praecentor of the college, the ministers of the several 17 parish churches, the register keepers of the several quakers' cemeteries, the several Anabaptists' cemeteries, the Jews' newly erected cemetery" for the ten years from 1741 to 1750. Using a figure of six people to a house he concluded that the Bristol population was 43,692 from the number of houses compared with 43,275 from the number of burials. Browning's results were communicated in 1753 by Henry Baker to the Royal Society who published [95] them in 1754. Population data were not Browning's only interest and he had earlier (12 September 1751) forwarded details to the Royal Society on Lewis Hopkin, a 15 year-old Welsh boy exhibited in Bristol who weighed thirteen pounds and was two feet seven inches tall.

In July 1752 a civil survey was undertaken in the city of Norwich. The numbers of married couples and the number of houses were included in the original returns which are in the Norfolk and Norwich Record Office. Price quoted [96] the numbers of families and inhabitants in his 'Observations'.

At Liverpool a survey of the number of houses was made in 1753; reference was made to this by Price alongside the Norwich enumeration of the previous year.

1753 should have been one of the major milestones in the history of British censuses. It was in this year that Thomas Potter, a son of the late Archbishop of Canterbury, introduced his Population Bill, putting some far-reaching proposals before Parliament. The tabled Bill was descriptively entitled 'A Bill, with the Amendments, for Taking and Registering an annual Account of the total Number of People, and the total Number of Marriages, Births and Deaths; and also the total Number of Poor receiving Alms from every Parish, and extraparochial Place, in Great Britain'. The opening paragraphs further explained: "Whereas it will be of publick Utility, that the total Number of People within this Realm, together with the progressive Increase or Diminution thereof, as either may respectively happen; and also the total Number of Poor receiving Alms from every Parish, or extraparochial Place; be annually taken and registered: And whereas great Inconveniencies have arisen from the present defective manner in which parochial Registers are formed, and the loose and uncertain Method in which they are kept and preserved; whereby the Evidence of Descents is frequently lost and rendered precarious:

Be it therefore enacted ...... the Overseers of the Poor, for the Time being, of every Parish, ... shall proceed from House to House to every House within their respective Parish or District; and shall demand and take an Account of the Number of People who at that time shall be, and, for the Space of Twelve Hours next preceding, shall have been, personally resident and actually dwelling therein ......"

Potter met with much opposition, not only within Parliament, and a number of pamphlets were published criticising his Bill. One, in particular, which was produced later in 1753 is worthy of note; running to several sheets, on the fifteenth page is stated : "You mention, that the ascertaining the Genealogy and Descents, may be of great Use; Our Ancestors did not think so; when they bought off the Courts of Ward, and, inquisitio post mortem, they looked upon this registering of every Man's Death and Birth by the Officers of the Crown, to be a high Badge of Slavery, and so destructive to the Liberties of a free People, that they gave Excise to get rid of this Egyptian Bondage; but you say they are only now obliged to register with the Parson of the Parish: And why so? Are we to give to the Priests what our Ancestors refused to the King? Why should the Dissenter register with the Parson of the Parish, and not with the Minister of his own Congregation? Why should not the Jew be allowed to register with his own Priest? Why should not the Nobility be allowed to register in the Herald's-Office? And as for Descent of the Poor, what need they to register? What signifies Genealogy to poor Labourers and Manufacturers, and they are twenty to one of those to whom Genealogy may be of Use, yet are all to pay to the Priest of the Parish? As for Successions, and the Times when Youth comes of Age, we find that they do take Possession of their Estates, and we find few Inconveniencies; and if some Disputes have arisen, a few Inconveniencies can be no Objection to a general Law, since no general Law can be without few Inconveniencies."

Correspondence in the 'Gentlemen's Magazine' during November and December 1753, led particularly by William Thornton, argued strongly against Potter's proposals (the support was permitted very little column space). But two arguments finally disposed of Potter's Bill: it was felt that a census and its published results would reveal England's weakness in terms of its population structure to her potential enemies, but more drastically the opponents recounted the fate of the Children of Israel as described in the First Book of Chronicles [97] in the Old Testament: when David had attempted to number the tribes - conduct a census - the wrath of God had been brought upon them. Having no wish to cause a similar fate to eighteenth century Great Britain, the 1753 Population Bill wavered and then when parliamentary time ran out it was abandoned.

But the seeds of interest had been sown, and after 1753 public debate on population figures for England and Wales intensified, so catalysing the enthusiasm for individuals to conduct either simple enumerations or even complex censuses in their locality.

In 1754, for example, a population survey was undertaken in the parish of Stockport, Cheshire by the ecclesiastical authorities. Religious affiliation and location in the parish were given on the original survey which is in the Bodleian Library. There is, however, a copy in Stockport Public Library and commentaries [98] have been published on this particular survey.

An 'Account of the Number of People in Scotland in the Year 1755' was prepared by Dr Alexander Webster, minister of Tolbooth Church, Edinburgh; however, it was not published until 1952 when James Gray Kyd's commentary on Webster's work appeared in one of the annual volumes of the Scottish History Society [99] . Kyd included a transcript of the census of the 892 parishes in Scotland. The census actually comprised a numerical analysis of ministers, papists, protestants and fighting men in each parish, for which the length and breadth were also stated. Whilst 1755 appears in Webster's title to his document, the original manuscripts of which are now in the National Library of Scotland, it is more likely that most of the population figures refer to 1750. Webster was in correspondence with Price in 1771 regarding this enumeration as demonstrated in Price's [100] 'Observations' (where he quoted estimated numbers of Papists and Protestants made "with labour and expence" by Rev Dr Webster) and confirmed by A J Youngson, who published a short article [101] on Webster and his census in 1962.

Rev William Brackenridge in London began some heated correspondence by publishing an article in the 'Philosophical Transactions of the Royal Society' [102] in 1755. He claimed that London's population had fallen since earlier that century, a claim later extended to the whole country. This was refuted by Rev Richard Forster of Great Shefford in Berkshire also in Philosophical Transactions; after a while the editors curtailed the claims and counter claims but the opponents continued their correspondence privately between themselves, occasionally involving third parties. Some of this correspondence has been deposited in the British Museum [103].

A survey taken at Stroud, Gloucestershire in 1756, which was quoted in 1779 by Samuel Rudder in his 'New History of Gloucestershire...', and that at Southampton taken in 1757, referred to in the Southampton Herald for 18 June 1825, may also have been initiated by the Royal Society's publication. In Belfast on 1 January 1757 a survey was undertaken of the number of looms, houses and inhabitants. This survey was referred to by Price [104] who revealed that of the population 7993 were Protestant and 556 were Papists. The 1757 enumeration of Ackworth, Yorkshire was probably associated with the debate; it was certainly quoted by William Wales [105] (see below, 1779 and 1781) and by Price [106] when the second phase of the national population arguments heated up from 1779 (qv). Price quoted the actual figures of inhabitants for males and for females in the age ranges: under 2, 2 to 5, 5 to 10, 10 to 20, and by ten-year groups to 90 to 100. The number of inhabitants in Speen in Berkshire was taken in 1757 and later quoted by Price [107].

On the other hand, publication on 21 March 1757 of the population figures for Hereford, listed by streets and also noting the numbers of houses as an inset to a map of the city was the work of Isaac Taylor. It was Taylor who had published the map of Oxford in 1751 bearing the population of that city, before the public debate had become inflamed.

Meanwhile central government had imposed a Silver Plate Tax in 1756, which remained on the Statute Book until 1777. The returns for this, which include the names of the taxpayers and the amounts they paid were deposited with the clerk to the county justices during the quarter sessions among which records they may be found today in county archives.

In 1757 it became necessary to introduce a new Militia Act as there were no competent persons left in the old county militia regiments to defend the local people in the event of an invasion, potentially by the French. All the professional soldiers were fighting on the continent in the relatively well organised armed forces established in 1660 as the new Standing Army. Those really interested in a military career had joined the army, leaving the old militia comprising only feeble amateurs. The 1757 Militia Act required that lists be made by counties in England and Wales of potential volunteers (men between 18 and 50) to serve in militia regiments. The clergy, teachers, apprentices, peace officers and peers were excluded. From the lists the actual recruits were picked by ballot; if they were unwilling or unable to serve they had to find a substitute - hence the initial lists have been termed Militia Ballot Lists, and the picked men appear on Militia Muster Rolls or Enrolment Lists. By the mid 1760s annual Ballot Lists were being prepared in most counties, the system being organised by the Privy Council through the county Lords Lieutenant and their deputies and the parish constables. The lists were, accordingly, collected by parishes into hundreds or wapentakes (or in some cases especially created sub-divisions); each hundred provided one Company for the county regiment of militia. Although not quarter sessions business, many county justices became involved in administering the balloting system and the lists are filed with quarter sessions records. In other instances the records remain among county lieutenancy papers or in some cases in private archives. Accepting that neither the Ballot Lists, the Muster Rolls nor the Enrolment Lists are censuses, and that several of the lists are far from complete, those that were carefully compiled do provide names of some of the men in certain localities between the ages of 18 and 50.

A dispute over mill rights in Manchester caused a census to be taken there in 1757. Whilst the population figure of 19,839 has survived, the original returns of this census do not appear to have done so. The existence of this census was referred to in the article 'Observations on the State of Population in Manchester and other adjacent Places ', which was published in the Philosophical Transactions of the Royal Society during 1774 [108]; the "observations" were made by Dr Thomas Percival although they were "communicated" to the Royal Society by Price.

A further Militia Act in 1758 required all males between 18 and 50 and their occupations to be listed; thus this year provides more names than did the previous year and further information on them as well. Some constables included the numbers of children under 10, or even their actual ages in their lists. Incidentally in 1762, by yet another Militia Act, the age range was altered to 18 to 45.

Another Bill for vital statistics was introduced before Parliament in 1758. Although no census as such was mentioned this was another attempt to take account of the question of a rising or falling population and the realisation that there was a definite lack of official statistics on which to base any accurate discussion. Like Potter's 1753 Population Bill, the 1758 one also failed.

In 1760 a census was taken at West Wycombe, Buckinghamshire. The original return is at the county record office in Aylesbury.

The detailed results of a census taken in 1762 at Whitehaven, Cumberland have been deposited in Whitehaven Public Library. The properties in the town and the occupations of the inhabitants were included in the return.

In 1764 an ecclesiastical survey of papists, parish by parish in the York Diocese was undertaken. The results may be found in a manuscript book, now cared for by the Borthwick Institute and filed with the Bishopthorpe manuscripts.

Another Cumberland census was undertaken in 1765, in this year for the town of Maryport. The returns for Maryport, which include occupations, are among the Benson records at Cockermouth Castle. The proportions of natives and strangers were included in the survey taken at Stratford-upon-Avon in 1765, although the main purpose of this census appears to have been to identify those who had suffered from smallpox. The findings were recorded by Robert Bell Wheler [109] in 1806 in his 'History and antiquities of Stratford upon Avon, comprising....'.

During this year the clergy in London and Westminster parishes were asked to supply information on papists, such as their numbers, where they met and the name of any Popish priests who were encouraging people in Popery in their parishes. Similar questions were asked in the following year. The responses for 1765 and 1766 are today with the Fulham Palace Papers [110] held by the Church Commissioners.

In 1767 a second survey (see 1757) for Ackworth, Yorkshire, was taken; on this occasion the numbers of houses - inhabited and uninhabited - were noted as well as the numbers of families and inhabitants. As in the case of the previous survey the 1767 results were referred to both by Price [111], who mentions a "curious register kept by Dr Lee", and by Wales.

Further lists of papists were required in 1767, but this time on a national basis, parish by parish, as a result of a resolution passed by the House of Lords on 22 May 1767. Throughout the country the clergy were asked to supply names, sexes, ages, occupations and length of time resident in each parish. Some returns are now in the House of Lords Record Office [112], some went to diocesan registries and have been passed on to county record offices and some are in Lambeth Palace Library. Several of the returns have been transcribed and published with commentaries, but for others only the summaries have survived.

For Newbury and adjoining Speen in Berkshire enumerations of the numbers of families and inhabitants were conducted in 1768. Although the whereabouts of the original returns are not now known, details of the survey were quoted by Price [113] and again a century later by Walter Money who gave figures for the districts in his 'History of the ancient town and borough of....Newbury, Berks....' published in 1887.

In 1770 enumerations were undertaken in the Devon parish of Okeford, the town (as it was then, and in Warwickshire) of Birmingham, distinguishing numbers of males and females, in Corsham and in Steeple Ashton, Wiltshire, in Liverpool and in Bury, Lancashire . The Okeford [114] figures of the numbers of inhabitants (422) and the Bury figures for houses and inhabitants were referred to by Price, whilst the Birmingham figures of the numbers of houses and inhabitants were quoted, not only by Price, but also in the 'Tradesmen's True Guide or a Universal Directory for the Towns of Birmingham, Wolverhampton, Walsall and Dudley', written in 1770 by Sketchley and Adam. The lists of names of the men and their occupations at Corsham and the inhabitants at Steeple Ashton have been deposited in the Wiltshire Record Office at Trowbridge. 1770 has already been mentioned (see 1700) as the last year during the eighteenth century when regular decennial enumerations were taken in Liverpool. The work of Dr Enfield on the population of Liverpool, apart from the commentaries of Price, and incidentally also of Howlett, is referred to below (see 1773).

At some time during this decade enumerations were conducted in Wiltshire at Calne, of families and inhabitants, and at nearby Bremhill, of houses and inhabitants. Whilst Price quoted [115] both of these, the present location of the original documentation is not known.

In 1771 at Swinderby, Lincolnshire the vicar, Dr Disney took a census, naming all his parishoners but he sent only the figures to Price. This census is now in the Lincolnshire Archives office [116]. In the same year an enumeration was taken at Leeds, Yorkshire. Both sets of figures were quoted

[117] by Price. The latter enumeration, together with another taken in 1775, was discussed at some length by Frank Beckwith in the 1948 publication of the Thoresby Society [118], comparing figures quoted earlier by Price and Wales. The work of Drs Lucas and Wood, analysing data in and around Leeds in the latter part of the eighteenth century was also discussed by Beckwith. In his 'Observations' Price quoted figures for the total inhabitants in the town of Leeds, the total in the villages and country near the town and the numbers of males, females, married persons, widows, widowers, unmarried males and unmarried females over 20 and girls and boys under 20. For 1775 a slightly different breakdown of the figures was quoted by Aikin in 1795 in his book (p 571) on Manchester (see 1781 below) who also added a gem of social history: "It is to be observed, that in the lowest rank of people there is often more than one family to a house".

On 1 January 1772 Rev Mr Travis, the vicar of Eastham, Cheshire and his uncle, the vicar of Royton, Lancashire, undertook "comprehensive censuses" (sic) in their respective parishes; the results of these were quoted by Dr Percival in his article [119] in 'Philosophical Transactions' in the 1774 issue, where he also attempted to relate death and disease to rainfall in that area of England. In March that year an accurate account was made of the numbers of houses, inhabitants and lodgers in part of St Pancras, London and later referred to by Price [120], as was that also taken during the year of the numbers of families and inhabitants in the village of Aldwinckle [121], Northamptonshire. In July and August, also in 1772, exact surveys were taken respectively in Altrincham, Cheshire and in the parish of St Mary, Chester; both were discussed in the Royal Society's 'Philosophical Transactions' for 1774, the former by Percival with the Eastham and Royton figures, the latter by Dr J Haygarth [122] who had taken the Chester survey himself anyway. Dr Haygarth's article, which also compared the Chester figures with those for Northampton, Norwich and London, was complemented by another [123] in 1778 concerning a subsequent survey of the whole of Chester which he undertook in 1774.

Also in 1772, in August, a listing was made at Cuxham, Oxfordshire, of all those inhabitants who had contracted small-pox. Those who had been given the disease by inoculation were distinguished on the listing from those who had otherwise caught it. The names were originally entered in the parish marriage register which commenced in 1754, now deposited in the county record office in Oxford.

Many local surveys were conducted in 1773 as interest on population figures spread throughout the country. In some cases names, ages and addresses are given on the surviving records, in other cases only the results as numbers appear. Some were at the direct request of Price or Percival, who have already been mentioned, to provide them with data for their arguments which they subsequently published. Other censuses seem to have been taken for local interest or information only, but most likely were inspired by the public debate taking place. The Bolton (with the suburb of Little Bolton), Lancashire, survey of April 1773 and those in Derbyshire at Chinley, Brownside and Bugsworth taken in September by Rev Mr Harrison of Chapel in le Frith were definitely for Percival's research; and he personally undertook a census of the Manchester and Salford townships in the summer of that year, referring to the results in his 1774 article mentioned above. For these two townships Percival quoted the numbers of houses, families, males, females, married persons, widowers, widows, those under 15 and those above 50, the male lodgers, the female lodgers and the empty houses - in fact almost every conceivable piece of information apart from the names of individuals in all the various categories. He even concluded that for Manchester and Salford there were six and two-fifth persons per house and four and a quarter individuals in a family from the total population of 27,246 - the sort of data that could usefully be woven into a social or family history for that area and period. In the same article Percival also referred to a census of Bury "just executed" and he quoted the results of a 1773 enumeration at Monton in the same county. Rev Mr Bolton, who helped collect some of the statistics in Monton for Percival, commented in words not unique to the eighteenth century that "drunkenness is more destructive to mankind, than pleurisies, fevers or the most malignant distempers".

Price also quoted [124] numbers of houses and inhabitants for Bolton and Little Bolton in his 'Observations' but he was able to add similar numbers for Chippenham, Wiltshire and for Liverpool, and for Manchester and Salford, adding only the numbers of families - not the full data of Percival. For Hale Chapel Price was able to refer to Percival's figures of males, females, married persons, widowers, widows and the totals for inhabitants under 15 and over 50 and to similar data for Mr Evans' congregation at Horwick, Rev Mr Smalley's congregation at Darwent and Rev Mr Barker's congregation at Cockey Moor. For Rev Mr Mercer's congregation at Chow-bent in Lancashire Price quoted numbers of males, females, married persons, widowers, widows, males under 10, females under 10, males over 50 and females over 50. Aikin also quoted many 1773 figures for houses and inhabitants in the thirty to forty mile radius from Manchester in his 1795 book (see 1781 below).

Although "survey" is the term most frequently used by Price, and he occasionally referred to a "census", particularly for his work on population during this decade little, if any, of the original documentation can now be found; this suggests that many of the figures were calculated from parish register entries rather than from house to house enquiries. However, the occasional reference to "a very accurate survey" or to one taken "with much labour" does indicate that a more rigorous census had been made, and hence the search today for the original documentation, possibly bearing names and further details on individuals is worthy of consideration.

Dr John Aikin was responsible for analysing the Bill of Mortality for Warrington, Lancashire for 1773, the results of which were published in 'Philosophical Transactions' [125]; in that article Aikin argued that as War-rington had 1600 to 1700 houses and with five persons per house the number of inhabitants was "somewhat above 8000" . Aikin also referred to the figures, but with no commentary, in his 1795 book on Manchester (see below under 1781). The Blandford Forum, Dorset, survey was obviously a direct result of the 'Philosophical Transactions' publicity, as details of the results from Blandford, which included an estimate of births to dissenters, were discussed by Dr Richard Pulteney in his article [126] which was published on its pages in 1778.

On the other hand the surveys of the populations of Bewdley, Wribbenhall and Kidderminster in Worcestershire were publicised by Treadway Russell Nash in his 'Collections for the history of Worcestershire', published be-tween 1781 and 1799 [127]. The 1773 enumeration of Liverpool was taken by Dr William Enfield, the results of which he published in 1774 with those taken every ten years from 1700 to 1770, in the second edition of his '.... history of Leverpool....' [128] , referred to above in conjunction with the 1700 enumeration. The figures were reproduced in 'Philosophical Transactions' [129] with a commentary on the huge increase in population of "Leverpool" from 5714 to 34004 during those seventy years.

The enumeration taken by the vicar of St Laurence, Ramsgate, Kent, and those which the same vicar took in 1785 and 1792 were referred to by William Boys in his 'Collections for an History of Sandwich in Kent....' published in 1792, and by Edward Hastead in his 'History and topographical survey of the County of Kent' in 1801 [130]. In June 1773 John Becher drew up "an accurate review of all the families in Renhold" in Bedfordshire with a "comprehensive account of their several characters which were searched into with indefatigable industry". This fascinating local census can be studied in the county archives [131] at Bedford.

On 17 April 1774 Colerne, Wiltshire was struck by a severe fire. A list was drawn up of the poor sufferers, their ages, their occupations and the value of their property. Although not a complete census, a list such as this, now in the record office at Trowbridge, may be of more value to a social or family historian than an unemotional survey or mere enumeration.

Price and Percival were almost as active in 1774 as in the previous year. Population figures of families and inhabitants for High Wycombe, Buckinghamshire were quoted by Price [132], and the 'Gentlemen's Magazine' for 1800 [133] published a report of the 1774 "very accurate account" of the inhabitants which was being taken at the request of Dr Price; however, the original document appears to have been lost. The local enumeration of the numbers of houses and inhabitants at Eastry, Kent is also quoted by Price [134]. Haygarth took a personal interest (Price stated that the survey was "made with great care under the direction of Dr Haygarth") in the population figures for the parishes including the suburbs of Chester in 1774 (see above under 1772); Haygarth's figures included families, inhabitants, males, females, married persons, widowers, widows, those under 15 and those over 50, numbers who "had recovered of, and those who had died of, the small pox" in 1774, and those who were ill of the small pox and those who had not had it in January 1775. Percival personally saw to the taking of an enumeration for the parish and the thirty-one townships for the whole of Manchester (as a sequel to his work of the previous year). The originals of the Manchester surveys are deposited in the library of Chetham College at Manchester University. Percival's commentary on these was published in 'Philosophical Transactions' for 1774 and 1775 [135]. Towards the end of his article in the latter year Percival quoted the numbers of males and of females in the townships of Manchester and Salford, in the parish of Manchester, in Bolton, Little Bolton, Monton, Hale, Horwich, Darwen, Cockey (Moor) (near Bolton), Chowbent, Ackworth, Eastham, Chinley, Brownside and Bugsworth. He also identified numbers of widowers and widows in the parish of Manchester and Salford, in the townships of each of these, and in Monton, Hale, Horwich, Darwen, Cockey, Chowbent, Chinley, and Brownside and Bugsworth.

Later in the 1775 volume of 'Philosophical Transactions' [136], in an article on 'Observations on the Difference between the Duration of Human Life in Towns and in Country Parishes and Villages', the names are given of several vicars who provided Price with data for that article; among the data are further population figures for other places, presumably taken in 1774 or before, although dates are not stated. Price duplicated the publication of some of these details in his own 'Observations'.

In yet another article in 1776 [137] in 'Philosophical Transactions', Percival referred to the August 1774 parish survey of Tattenhall, Cheshire taken by its curate, and to the survey taken in the same month by the incumbent at Waverton, also in Cheshire. Price elaborated [138] slightly in his 'Observations' by stating that the survey of these two parishes provided numbers of males, females and the total population above the age of 14. Price additionally quoted an enumeration of the families and inhabitants in Bala, Wales also conducted in 1774.

1775 saw the conducting of at least six local enumerations: that at Leeds has already been referred to (see 1771) . The results from Ashton under Lyne were quoted by Aikin in his 1795 book (p 228) on Manchester (see 1781 below), by Percival in his 1776 article (qv), and by Price who broke the results down into: total population, males, females, total married, those under 5, 5 to 10, 10 to 20, 20 to 50, 50 to 70 and 70 to 90. That at Beaminster, Dorset was taken in conjunction with the parish rates and the original can be consulted at the Dorset Record Office at Dorchester. At Cirencester, Gloucestershire an exact count of the population for that year was published in Rudder's work on Gloucestershire (see the Stroud survey for 1756). The Corporation of Salisbury was responsible for taking the census in that city in 1775 which included the relative numbers of strangers to natives; the results of this survey were included in 'Salisbury' by R Benson and H Hatcher, published in 1883. At Sandford in Devon, 1775 was the first of five years (the others were 1783, 1790, 1793 and 1800) when censuses with names of individuals were recorded. The originals are now in the Devon Record office at Exeter with other Sandford parish records.

6. Eighteenth century listings - 1776 to 1786

Evidently there was only one local survey undertaken in 1776, the year of the American Revolution, and that was at Sandwich, Kent. This did not escape Price's beady eye, however, and he referred [139] to it, quoting Boys' work (see 1773) which included the numbers of houses and persons in the town incorporating those in three workhouses and two hospitals.

In 1777 a national tax was introduced on Male Servants whereby households employing them had to pay the levy. It was, accordingly, not a census as such and in the majority of cases the servants are not named although the households are clearly identified; but it does enable comparisons to be made nationally, in contrast to the profusion of local surveys being conducted in this decade. A most complex scale of charges was applied depending on whether the servant was married or single, whether he was employed as a book-keeper, steward, warehouseman, waiter, groom, or stable-keeper, and whether he was let for hire, if in livery or not. Servants engaged in husbandry, manufacture or any trade were exempt as were those employed by the Royal Family or those in service at Oxford or Cambridge Universities or at the public schools of Westminster, Eton and Winchester. Male servants at some hospitals and those of naval or army personnel below officer rank were also exempt. Army or naval officers who were disabled or who were on half-pay were additionally exempt. This tax remained in force until 1852. The Society of Genealogists holds the returns for 1780 which give the names of 24,750 people paying this tax on 50,000 un-named servants.

There appear to have been special surveys in 1777 of houses, and in some cases of inhabitants, on which Price believed reliance could be placed; those in Suffolk which he particularly mentioned [140] were Beccles, Bungay, Henham, Sollerton, Shipmeadow, Weston, Wenbaston, Southwold, Aldeburgh, Orford and Gorlestone; Price also quoted figures collected by Wales for Westhall, Wangford, Holton, Spexhall, Swilland, Tuddenham, Westerfield, Wisset, Witnesham, Blythford and Bramfield in Suffolk and Ashill,

Clapton, Ilminster and Wayford in Somersetshire. There was an accurate survey, under the direction of Dr Bisset, of houses and inhabitants at Skelton in Yorkshire, quoted by Price [141] and the exact survey for Evesham was quoted in Nash's work on Worcestershire [142] (see the 1773 surveys which were undertaken in Worcestershire). A Maidstone, Kent survey was quoted by Price [143] in his debate on the differences between cottages and houses. Figures also for London, Thaxted, Essex, two other (unnamed) parishes in Essex and one (also unnamed) in Kent and for Northampton, Chester and Shrewsbury in 1777 were also used by Price in his arguments - again quoting from returns of window tax surveyors or other special surveys.

In 1778 a survey of the houses and population of the Bedfordshire parish Podington and its hamlet of Hinwick was undertaken, the results of which were communicated in 1782 by the vicar, Oliver St John Cooper, to John Nicholls who incorporated them into his 'Collections towards the History and Antiquities of Bedfordshire'. Cooper became vicar of Thurleigh in 1784 and in 1788 undertook a similar survey there, and also another for Podington (and separately for Hinwick) and yet another for his neighbouring birthplace, Milton Ernest. The originals of the 1788 surveys which include surnames and some Christian names are in the British Library (Add. Ms. 34383 pp 43-45); they were transcribed by the County Archivist, Chris Pickford and published in 1987[144]. The numbers of families and inhabitants in Worsley, Parton, Pendleton, Pendlebury and Clifton (all in Lancashire) in 1778 were quoted by Price [145] in his 'Observations'.

Examples of censuses that were taken in Scotland on particular estates for specific purposes are those of 1779 and 1792 [146] for the Duke of Argyll in Kyntyre. Although the former year was really an enumeration of tenants on the estates on mainland and insular Argyll, for each farm the listing does provide the number of resident families, the numbers of tacksmen, tacksmen's sons, the servants and cottars, but not the total population for each farm; a transcript of the 1779 listing was prepared by E R Cregreen of the Extra-mural Department of Glasgow University. The listing for 1792 is more valuable for family historians as it gives the total population on each farm by name and age. A useful commentary on how these censuses can be used to analyse the areas of settlement, range of ages and social status was written by Alan Gailey [147] from the Department of Geography at Glasgow University in 1960.

A survey of houses, families and inhabitants, as a result of a most unusual situation was conducted in Nottingham in September 1779: a party of unnamed gentlemen became involved in a wager causing a public subscription to be raised to pay for this survey to be undertaken. The results were published by Robert Lowe of Oxton in 1798 in an appendix to the second edition of his 'General View of the Agriculture of the County of Nottingham' [148]. The Rev Mr Wilson, vicar of Biddulph, Staffordshire undertook an accurate survey of the families and inhabitants by males and females within his parish in April 1779; his original survey, which names the householders, is in the County Record Office [149]. Wilson sent the figures from his survey to Dr Haygarth at Chester and they were also quoted by Price [150]. Additionally in that year G Young [151] gave details of the numbers of houses and inhabitants of Worcester in his 'Plan of the City and Suburbs of Worcester'. 1779 was memorable in Wembworthy, Devon, as a census of the population with their ages, was also undertaken there that year; the returns are now in the East Devon Record Office [152].

It was during 1779 that Rev Richard Price added further fuel to the population debate by publishing his 'Essay on the Population of England and Wales', initially as an appendix to 'The Doctrine of Annuities and Assurances on Lives and Survivorships' written by his nephew, William Morgan, the actuary to the Equitable Assurances Society. Hidden at the end of Morgan's learned work, Price's essay which concluded that the population of the country taken as a whole was falling, did not make an immediate impact; but the following year Price published his essay separately and the public argument burst into flame.

William Eden, first Lord Auckland, and a well respected public figure and politician, criticised Price straight away in a new edition of his 'Four Letters to the Earl of Carlisle' which he produced the same year. During the subsequent year, 1781, William Wales a mathematics teacher at Christ's Hospital, London and an astronomer who had accompanied Cook on his Pacific voyages, produced 'An Inquiry into the Present State of Population in England and Wales' and Rev John Howlett, vicar of Great Badow, and concurrently also of Dunmow in Essex, published 'An Examination of Dr Price's Essay on the Population of England and Wales'. Howlett concluded that the population was rising, in stark contrast to Price's thesis. Price was, however, ready to fight off his critics. He had a strong personality and was a forceful Presbyterian preacher, well-loved and respected not only by his London congregations but also by those who read his literary contributions to eighteenth century society. And so Price's essay went into another edition in 1780 with an appendix to answer his critics. Further editions of his Essay, and also of his earlier work 'Observations on Reversionary Payments', were used in the counter-attack. As discussed above it is obvious that not a few of the locally conducted surveys were taken at the request of Price or one of his opponents to glean evidence on the population figures for one side or the other of the ensuing discussions.

Land tax in some form or other had been applied since 1692 and remained viable until 1831, but in 1780 the arrangements for its administration were changed. From this year the assessment returns had to be sent to the Clerk of the Peace for the immediate county at the Spring Quarter Sessions. Thus from 1780 the original returns, where they survive, are with the Quarter Sessions records in county record offices. There is, additionally an almost complete set of returns covering the whole country, but only for the year 1798, in the Public Record Office [153]. The documents for this particular year have probably survived because from 1798 land owners were able to make a once off payment to enable them to be exonerated from further liability to pay the annual tax, and it was necessary to have a complete national listing of land owners and occupiers. As mentioned above, prior to 1780 these returns may be found in a variety of archive depositories. The tax was assessed on the real and personal estate of persons owning land having an annual value of above twenty shillings, and also on certain public salaries and pensions. Thus poorer people were exempt and were not included on the lists. The assessment system was supervised by county commissioners, who appointed parish assessors and collectors. Even tenants paid this tax but they deducted it from their rents; thus most assessment lists have the names of landlords and tenants. The amount paid, which should have been calculated at the rate of four shillings in the pound, was shown on the returns alongside the names of the owners and occupiers of the houses and land. This data is useful to the social and family historian to give an indication of the economic status of a named individual. Several of these land tax assessment lists have been transcribed and published by local historical, antiquarian, and archaeological societies.

An enumeration at Farnham, Surrey undertaken in 1780 was referred to during the following year by William Wales [154] in his 'Inquiry'. The original documents of the Farnham survey have not been traced, nor have those of the "exact survey" of houses in Christleton, Lancashire, referred to by Price [155].

In 1780, for the second time on a national basis (see 1767) lists of papists were made parish by parish. These were in response to an address from the House of Lords on 3 July 1780. Although not demanded by the Archbishops of Canterbury and York, many returns include names, ages, sexes, occupations and the length of time resident in the parish. Some returns give initials rather than names, thus providing the Catholic researcher with an interesting challenge. Many originals are in the House of Lords Record Office [156] but the results have been listed in the Journal of the House of Lords [157]. The parish returns for the London Diocese are held by the Catholic Record Society [158] and some incumbents' original returns, formerly in diocesan registries, are now in county record offices.

In 1781 Dr Aikin obtained another enumeration of the houses and inhabitants of the town and township of Warrington, including Poulton, Fearnhead and Woolston, (see 1773), the results of which he included in 'A description of the country from thirty to forty miles round Manchester; containing...', published in 1795. This survey was mentioned by Price as providing numbers of inhabitants and houses, inhabited and uninhabited, as were two of Maidstone, Kent [159] one of houses, families and inhabitants taken the same year and another the next year, 1782 (qv). Two surveys were taken in Wiltshire in 1781, one at Swindon, the other at Warminster. The former [160] was quoted by Price, the latter [161] in the 1965 edition of the Victoria County History of Wiltshire, but the whereabouts of the originals of both these surveys are now unknown.

The 'General Account of the number of persons in each house' in the village of Cardington, Bedfordshire was taken on 1 January 1782, probably by the schoolmaster, James Lilburne. The original returns, which name every inhabitant, their ages, relationships in each house, occupations and other details, are in the county record office in Bedford. However, a most comprehensive annotated transcript was prepared by David Baker and published by the Bedfordshire Historical Record Society in 1973, as mentioned in the preface. Also in Bedfordshire, Rev Richard How of Aspley Guise entered into correspondence with John Howlett in Essex regarding the population of Aspley. How examined his parish registers from 1563 and the Poor Law expenditure within the parish. The original correspondence has been deposited in the local county archives [162], but was also quoted by Baker in his work on the detailed census of Cardington.

Additionally in January 1782 a second survey of Belfast (see 1757) indicated the numbers of houses, numbers of inhabitants, male and female, the number of looms and the number of houses selling beer and spirits. Price referred to this survey in his 'Observations' [163].

The September 1782 survey of Maidstone, Kent, which was referred to by Price with that of the year before, was published in 1782 as a pamphlet 'Observations on the Increased Population, Healthiness, etc of the Town of Maidstone'. However, the author's name was not published and whilst Price attributed this census to John Howlett, the Essex vicar mentioned above, it was also attributed to the curate of Maidstone, Rev J Deane, by J M Russell in his 'History of Maidstone....' published in 1881. The original pamphlet kept at Maidstone Museum details the numbers of families, houses and male and female inhabitants; male servants, female servants, women above 70, men above 70, girls under 15 and boys under 15 were separately enumerated in the town and in the country.

In the Autumn of 1782 "a very accurate survey" was made of the inhabited and uninhabited houses in Birmingham; but only their numbers, not their occupants or owners, appear to have survived. These numbers are quoted by Price [164].

Dr William White undertook a survey of York as a contribution to the population debate, publishing [165] his interpretation of the results in 'Philosophical Transactions' in 1782.

The Minehead, Somerset, survey of 1783, similarly to that of 1705 (qv), was referred to in 1791 by John Collinson in his 'History....of Somerset'. The Sandford, Devon census of 1783 has been mentioned (see 1775).

In 1784 a tax on horses, mares, geldings and mules, whether used for riding (including racing) or drawing carriages or in husbandry, was levied nationally. The levy varied enormously depending on the use to which the horses were put, pleasure horses being taxed at 57s 6d whilst the duty on husbandry horses was 3s each. A butcher using a horse when carrying out his trade had to pay the same high rate as for a racehorse whereas a bailiff in using a horse for his duties paid only 50s a year. The duty on horses above thirteen hands high was greater than on smaller horses. There were certain exemptions: "horses used in husbandry, or drawing any carriage not liable to duty, or carrying burdens in the course of trade or occupation of the person to whom such horse shall belong, if rode only when going for a load, or returning, or going for medical assistance, or to or from any market, or place of public worship, election of members of parliament, or to or from any court of justice, or to or from any meeting of commissioners of taxes". All this meant that anyone possessing horses had to pay the sum annually (unless the exemptions could be applied), with the result that the taxation lists, which for most counties are filed with the quarter sessions records, provide useful sources of names and enable more pictorial information to be added to a family or social history. This tax remained on the statute books until 1874.

Another national levy imposed in 1784 was the Game Duty Tax. All persons who wished to kill or even to sell game - and for the purposes of this tax woodcock, snipe, quail, landrail and coney were also included - were obliged to have licences. These were issued annually, taking effect from 6 April each year, in every county by the Clerks of the Peace in exchange for a monetary payment. Manorial gamekeepers were not exempted from this levy, which demonstrates the further decline of the influence of ancient manorial rights and the rise in importance of county administration. Nevertheless there were exemptions for those who caught woodcocks or snipes with nets or springs, or those who caught coneys in warrens or enclosed grounds; furthermore, no tax was payable by persons who caught game on their own land with ferrets or nets. The Game Duty Tax remained in force until 1807. The lists of those who paid were filed with the quarter sessions records within each county.

A survey of Lancaster was taken by Thomas Batty the parish clerk in 1784. A statistical analysis is now in the corporation archives. Batty's work was publicised by C Clark in 1807 when he reproduced the data in 'An Historical and Descriptive Account of the Town of Lancaster'. An accurate account (the contemporary wording) of the population of Great Yarmouth, Norfolk during 1784 was referred to in his 'Notices of Great Yarmouth' by J H Drury, published in 1826. The original account has not been located. Also in 1784 enumerations were undertaken in Westmorland of Kendal, Kirkby Lonsdale,

Sedburgh and Burton in Kendal. The original documents appear not to have survived although the results were published in 'Local Chronology' in 1865 and Sir Frederick Morton Eden referred to the Kendal figures in his 'State of the Poor' [166] which was published in 1797. Sir Frederick, a nephew of William Eden (see 1779), was particularly interested in life expectancy rates and the type of information which could be predicted from Bills of Mortality - in fact he was one of the founders and subsequently Chairman of the Globe Insurance Company.

A tax was imposed on a nation-wide basis in 1785 on all households employing female servants, similar to that imposed on male servants in 1777 (qv). The Female Servants Tax, sometimes referred to as the Maid Servants Tax, remained in force until 1792.

Locally in 1785 an enumeration of the numbers of families and souls was undertaken in Leicester. The results were quoted in 1791 by John Throsby in his 'History and antiquities of....Leicester', but no original documents survive. A detailed census undertaken for Frome, Somerset, which was referred to by both Collinson [167] and Eden [168] is now in private hands, but there are copies at Somerset Record office and Frome Museum. The census names the householders and their occupations and lists the numbers of males and females in each house. With future historical researchers obviously in mind the census names the owner of every house, the number of scribblers and shearmen in each, the numbers of looms owned by weavers, and the number of cows kept by each householder. A list of the inhabitants of the Wiltshire parish of Little Cheverall, also taken during 1785, may be consulted at the county record office in Trowbridge. The Ramsgate census undertaken by the vicar has already been mentioned (see 1773).

7. Listings from 1787

A list of the inhabitants of Chisleden, Wiltshire, was made on 15 February 1787; the original list is in the Wiltshire County Record Office at Trowbridge. At quarter sessions in both Cumberland and Westmorland in 1787 all parishes were asked to conduct a local census and forward the returns to the Clerks of the Peace. The majority of the original documents for Westmorland parishes have been deposited in the county archives at Kendal with the quarter sessions records - but for Cumberland enumerations only for Carlisle appear to have survived. Also for Carlisle are the 'Observations on the Bills of Mortality' published annually by J Heysham from 1779 to 1787, the last year containing the figures requested by the quarter sessions. The original observations from 1781 to 1787 are housed in the public library at Carlisle, but were summarized by both Henry Lonsdale [169] and William Hutchinson [170] later in the eighteenth century.

On 1 April 1788 the States Parliament on Jersey, in response to a request from the English Parliament, ordered a survey of the island. The instructions were to list the numbers of men, women and children both present and absent; however, the authorities in the parish of St Lawrence interpreted the ordinance further and on 9 April 1788 made lists of the names of all the parishioners with their ages, by vingtaines (sub-divisions of parishes). These lists are extremely useful to family historians, as with many Jersey records, because wives are listed with their maiden surnames. For the other parishes only population numbers appear to have been taken. The original returns are in the La Société Jersiaise Library, but transcripts of the St Lawrence lists were published by the Channel Islands Family History Society [171] in 1980, 1981 and 1982.

During 1788 James Pilkington was active in Derbyshire, either conducting or initiating surveys in at least twenty-one parishes in the county. In the second edition of his 'A View of the Present State of Derbyshire with an account of its most remarkable antiquities....', published in 1803, Pilkington quoted the "exact enumeration" of Chesterfield [172], taken in December 1788 and the "actual enumeration" of Derby - which he took personally during 1788. Statistical analyses of many other parishes were also included in the same work. Dr Percival, who had promoted the taking of enumerations in and around Manchester since the early 1770s (qv), took a further survey of Manchester township in 1788. The results of that survey were published as an appendix to his 'Essays, Medical, Philosophical and Experimental' when it was reprinted in 1807. The figures for an enumeration of 1788 for the parish of Harrington, Cumberland, were incorporated in the Visitation Returns of 1788-9 of the Chester diocese. The original returns are in the Chester Record Office.

In October 1789 an accurate count of Burton upon Trent, Staffordshire, was made, according to the 'History and Antiquities of Staffordshire, ...including Erdwick's Survey....' by Stebbing Shaw [173]; however, the original documents cannot now be traced. A similar situation pertains for the originals of the enumeration taken of Bolton, Lancashire during 1789 which was referred to by Aikin (see 1781).

Between 1789 and 1793 the population figures for many Nottinghamshire parishes were obtained by going from house to house. The figures were quoted by Lowe [174] in his 'General View...', referred to above, in conjunction with the 1779 survey of Nottingham. It is believed that another census of Nottingham was taken in 1793; according to Lowe the expenses incurred to undertake it were certainly paid for by Sir Richard Sutton, although the returns themselves appear to be missing today. However, a census for West Retford taken in 1794 has survived and is in the county archives.

In the Devon parishes of Sandford and Tiverton censuses were undertaken in 1790. The original returns of the former have been mentioned above (see 1775). For the latter an enumeration only was made in January of that year and quoted by Martin Dunsford in his 'Historical Memoirs of the town and parish of Tiverton....' [175].

A census of Corfe Castle for 1790 which included names, ages, conditions (married, bachelor etc), occupations and probable weekly incomes and paid by whom, was referred to [176] by Rev John Hutchins the rector of Wareham in his work on Dorset. This census also recorded by sex, the housekeepers, children and grandchildren resident with their parents, lodgers and inmates, servants and apprentices, and their addresses and names, ages and occupations.

In October of the same year at Hayes, Kent a list of the parishioners, household by household, was compiled by Rev John Till, the rector. Several households include the names of lodgers who do not appear in the parish registers, and the occupations of many of the individuals are given. This list, which was formerly among Till's papers in the Kent County Archives, is now housed [177] at Bromley Reference Library in Kent.

Also during 1790 Dr Joshua Toulmin went from house to house in Taunton, Somerset to collect data on the population which he published both in his own 'History of Taunton in the county of Somersetshire' [178] and also as an article [179] in the 'Monthly Magazine and British Register', a London-based periodical. Toulmin's separate 'History....' was later enlarged by J Savage and G Webb and reprinted in 1874.

At Swinderby, Lincolnshire, a similar census to that of 1771 (qv) was undertaken in 1791. The original returns are in the county archives [180].

The 1792 survey of Ramsgate, Kent has already been referred to above (see 1773 and 1785). At Kingston upon Hull, Yorkshire a census was taken during 1792 by the Society for Literary Information. This was referred to by J Ticknell in his 'History of the Town and County of Kingston upon Hull' [181], published in 1796, and also by Eden [182]. The Gentlemen, Farmers and inhabitants of Rugby (1553 of them) signed a Declaration of attachment to the King and Constitution in 1792. The original is in Warwickshire Record office [183].

A nation-wide tax was imposed in 1793 on all holders of armorial bearings and remained in force until 1882. The tax was assessed at three levels: those who had a carriage had to pay more than those who did not, presumably because the achievement was seen by a wider audience by virtue of being displayed on the carriage. Those who also paid house duties, but who did not have a carriage, paid a lower tax than those who had a carriage - but they paid a higher tax than those who had neither carriage nor the obligation to pay house duties. The Armorial Bearings Tax was payable to the Clerk to the County Justices and the lists of those who paid and the amounts were filed with the quarter sessions records for the relevant county.

A locally conducted census of the Essex parish of Bocking in 1793 may be consulted at the county record office in Chelmsford. The Kendal survey for this year appears to have been taken under similar circumstances as that for 1784 (qv). It is quoted by Eden [184], but the original returns do not appear to have survived. The Sandford, Devon census was referred to above (see 1775).

In 1794 local surveys were conducted at Cambridge, Stockton upon Tees in Durham, West-Retford in Nottinghamshire (see 1789), Brighton in Sussex and Skipton in Yorkshire. The Cambridge population figures may be found with the Bowtell Manuscripts at Downing College, Cambridge, with those for 1749 (qv). Reference to the Stockton census was made in Rev John Brewster's 'Parochial History and Antiquities of Stockton upon Tees....' [185] published in 1829 although the original documents appear to have been lost; Brewster was rector of Egglescliffe. The Brighton survey was conducted prior to an inoculation campaign in the town and was referred to by Charles Wright [186] in 'The Brighton Ambulator....' in 1818 as being an exact enumeration. The Skipton census recorded some 2096 inhabitants in the town and identified the numbers of families as well; the whereabouts of the original returns are now unknown.

A national duty on the use of Hair Powder was introduced on 5 May 1795; the powder itself was already the subject of a tax from an earlier law. Each individual who used hair powder was required to pay a guinea and in return received an annual licence although payment for two unmarried daughters exempted the rest of the household from the dues. Clergymen of any denomination who had an annual income of less than £100 were exempt from paying this tax, as were ranks below officer in the navy, army or militia, and members of the Royal Family and their servants. A gentleman was able to take out a licence for his butler, coachman, footman etc and if he changed them during the year, the licence stood good for the newly engaged servants. About 200,000 people paid this tax in the first year which encouraged Pitt, who had introduced the Bill, to have it raised to £1 3s 6d per head. There was, however, opposition to the principle of this levy causing cropping and combing out of the hair to become fashionable. The Duke of Bedford was foremost in leading this fashion, followed swiftly by many of the gentry, and then lower strata of society, initially in Bedfordshire. By 1869 only about £1000 per annum was raised from approximately 800 individuals paying this duty and thus it was repealed that year.

In July 1795 a census, household by household, was conducted in the parish of St Andrew Worcester - sometimes termed the "Tanners' and Glovers' parish". The original returns are in the county record office in Worcester.

A survey of the houses and inhabitants at Uley in Gloucestershire was undertaken in about 1795 by Michael Lloyd-Baker's great grandfather; he made a rough plan of the village in his estate pocket book and allocated a number to each of the 299 houses. Against every number, on a separate schedule, he listed both Christian and surnames of the occupants. When Michael Lloyd-Baker wrote 'The Story of Uley' around 1910 he reproduced [187] after the first edition the sketch map and the associated list of names so enabling us to discover not only know who was in the village but exactly where they all lived. Also in 1795 a a detailed survey, including occupations, was conducted in Epsom, Surrey; the results without names were published in some depth by Eden [188].

In 1796 John Rickman wrote a memorandum on behalf of George Rose, the MP for Christchurch, Hampshire, on the potential advantages of conducting a general enumeration of the people of the British Empire. This was sent to Charles Abbot, the MP for Helston, Cornwall. This event, in itself, may not appear particularly significant - there had, after all, been many similar suggestions over the years. But it should be noted that when Abbot later became Chief Secretary and Privy Seal in Ireland he chose Rickman as his secretary, and four years later Abbot and Rickman achieved what scores of other advocates of a national census had failed to do when Parliament accepted their proposals.

A Dog Tax, applicable on a national basis, was introduced during 1796 and remained in force until 1882. When first administered this tax was quite complicated because of the sliding scales related to the breed of dog and the purpose for which it was kept. Greyhounds, for example were taxed at a higher rate than spaniels, lurchers or terriers, and other breeds were at a lower rate still. Whelps under six months were exempt. A pack of fox hounds could be taxed collectively. A licence was issued in return for the annual tax paid and fines were payable for those who failed to purchase a licence.

In Carlisle in 1796 a further survey was conducted (see 1787). The results were published by Hutchinson in 1796 with those for 1781 to 1787 as mentioned above.

In 1797 at Harlow in Essex a census was undertaken locally, the original returns of which have been deposited in the Essex Record Office at Chelmsford.

As a direct consequence of the Napoleonic Wars at the end of the seventeenth century the British Parliament introduced a Defence of the Realm Act in 1798. This was designed to identify all men throughout the country between the ages of 15 and 60 who were not at that time involved in any military activities. The aim was to locate potential recruits for the Posse Comitatus (Home Guard) should the French be successful in landing on British soil. In every parish of each county parish constables were required to record the names and occupations of all able-bodied men in the stated age bracket and to specifically identify the millers, bakers and wagon and barge owners. Unfortunately very few of these lists survive for most counties, and where they do they are in a variety of locations. There is a complete set for Buckinghamshire in the Stowe Manuscripts Collection at the British Museum, although the returns for the county (from a slightly different copy in the county archives) have been edited and usefully indexed [189] with an interesting background commentary by Dr Ian Beckett. Those few for Northamptonshire are in the County Record Office in Northampton; for other counties JSWG has indicated [190] where these lists may be found.

It is likely that the 1798 Act caused the authorities at Stockton upon Tees in County Durham to conduct the census there in 1799 which was referred to by Brewster (see 1794); the Stockton listing was, therefore, not a true census but a Posse Comitatus list. As the original material is now lost and only Brewster's reference survives we shall never know for certain.

In 1800, at Melbury Osmond in Dorset a local census was undertaken, very much on the same lines as the censuses which were conducted throughout the remainder of the nineteenth century; in fact this census has often erroneously been attributed to 1801, the style being so similar to subsequent surveys. The original returns are now in the Dorset Record Office. The census taken at Sandford, Devon during this year was referred to above (see 1775).

Finally in 1800, as a result of the lobbying, the public debate, the pamphlets and the correspondence another Population Bill was laid before Parliament; Abbot, to whom Rickman had written four years previously, introduced the Bill on 19 November 1800 and this time the attempt was a success, the Bill coming into force during the following year. Thus a nation-wide census was held on 10 March 1801 and a similar national enumeration has taken place every ten years since then (except in 1941 when Britain was otherwise busy). Rickman was made responsible for organising the 1801 census which was taken through local parish officers - in fact the parish overseers who remained responsible for the registration of electors, and a number of other duties associated with censuses, until the Representation of the People Act of 1918. Rickman, with the national figures available to him, which included information derived from parish registers prior to 1801, was able to compile various statistical analyses of the census results and then estimate the growth of the nation's population through the seventeenth and eighteenth centuries.

Even the regular, decennial censuses henceforth imposed on every community in the country did not diminish enthusiasm in some areas for conducting local surveys and enumerations and listings of inhabitants; on some occasions with details of names, ages, addresses, occupations and other details which were not requested on a national basis until much later in the nineteenth century.

For example, there was the September 1806 census of Jersey, ordered by the Lieutenant Governor, containing 4363 names of heads of families and numbers of men, women, boys and girls; the original returns are in the Jersey Government Office but there are copies which have been indexed by the Channel Islands Family History Society in La Societe Jersiaise Library and in their own library. There was the 1817 survey by Rev Henry Comyn in Hampshire of the combined parishes Boldre and Brockenhurst into which he incorporated sketch maps of the locations of houses, exact dates of birth of many parishoners, schools which some children were attending and other intimate details; the original manuscript notes are held by Hampshire County Library Service, but an illustrated, indexed transcription by Jude F James was published in 1982 [191]. There was the 1825 census of Hungerford, Berkshire taken on 1 January that year; it names the heads of households and their children but not the names of their wives. As it was updated in 1826, 1833, 1834 and 1835 and separate revisions were prepared in 1828, 1829, 1830 and 1831, all of the which are in the Berkshire Record Office, Donald Steel [192] believes these censuses were connected with outdoor relief under the poor laws. There was the 1832 listing, now in the county archives, [193] of the inhabitants of Summertown, Oxford on behalf of the incumbent, but with some marvellous uninhibited biographical comments by J Badcock. There was the 1834-36 analysis of Bowerchalke, Wiltshire, which gave not only names of the inhabitants but for each their date and place of birth, baptism and marriage. There was the 1837 census of Houghton Conquest in Bedford-shire, the original documents [194] of which are in that county's archives.

In 1803 two Defence Acts were passed by Parliament in a further attempt (see the 1798 Defence Act) to anticipate civil defence procedures needed should the French invade Britain. Levee en Masse lists were required to be drawn up by the parish constables. The first Act in June sought the same details as the 1798 Act; but the second Act in July 1803 required the equivalent of a complete census of the entire population by name, on a variety of schedules which requested many other personal details. Many of the schedules have not survived, or possibly were never completed, but the information required on the first schedule was the name, age, occupation, marital status, infirmity and number of children under ten years of age for each male between the ages of 17 and 55; on the second schedule the names of all householders, their ages and occupations, whether they were quakers or aliens, and how many males and females there were in those households; on the third schedule the non-combatants who would require evacuating had to be listed by name, age and occupation - in practice this implied the women, children, old and infirm; the fourth schedule comprised men between 17 and 55 who would form the pioneers and special constables; the fifth schedule listed the purveyors and carriers of strategic supplies, such as millers, bakers, wagon and barge owners, guides, wagoners, stockmen and the numbers of stock and amounts of fodder that would have also to be moved in the event of an invasion. For some counties digests were made of these complex schedules; only summaries of the figures have survived for other counties, among the Lieutenancy papers and Privy Council records. Most of the original schedules were retained by those who completed them and so disappeared either into private collections or were destroyed; the present whereabouts of any of these would be welcome.

What has been described as a 'Don's Military Census' was conducted on Jersey in 1815 by parishes on the orders of Lieutenant General Don, the

Commander in Chief and also the Lieutenant Governor of the Island. However, the document contains not only names, ages, and ranks in the militia but also names and (some) occupations of all men from 17 to 80 and the numbers of women, boys and girls. The names are listed alphabetically in each vingtaine of the twelve parishes on the Island. The original census is in the Jersey Government Office but there are copies in the libraries of La Société Jersiaise and the Channel Islands Family History Society.

The information required for the 1801, 1811 and subsequent decennial censuses prior to 1841 has already been mentioned at the beginning of this cameo. But, as discussed before, for a variety of reasons additional details were collected and recorded for a number of parishes and registration districts. Some of these are identified in Appendix II which follows. The author would welcome others being drawn to his attention.

In conclusion it should not be overlooked that whilst specific towns or parishes, for which lists of individuals' names were made, are identified in Appendix I, there were in addition many national surveys for taxation or religious or military purposes which contain names of people. Researchers are accordingly urged to refer to such surveys described in this cameo at the locations indicated. The appropriate archivist will be able to advise on the availability of these pre-1841 censuses and population listings.

Appendix I - Censuses referred to in the main text containing names of individuals

The years for which there are listings for an entire county are given first, in chronological order, followed by listings in alphabetical order for specific areas of that county. The existence of a nineteenth century decennial census in a county is indicated last but by the year only; the exact areas covered by these can be found in Appendix II.

Aberdeenshire	1695.
Bedfordshire	1297; Cardington 1782; Hinwick 1778, 1788; Houghton Conquest 1837; Milton Ernest 1788; Pavenham 1699; Podington 1778, 1788; Renhold 1773; Thurleigh 1788; 1811, 1821, 1831.
Berkshire	Hungerford 1825-1835; 1801, 1811, 1821, 1831.
Buckinghamshire	1798; West Wycombe 1760; 1801, 1811, 1821, 1831.
Caernarvonshire	1597.
Cambridgeshire	Cambridge 1749; Diocese of Ely 1716-44; 1801, 1811, 1821.
Cheshire	1723; Diocese of Chester 1705; 1821, 1831.
Cornwall	1334-1434.
Cumberland	Carlisle 1377, 1787, 1796; Maryport 1765; Whitehaven 1762.
Derbyshire	1633; Melbourne 1695; 1801.
Derry	1831.

Devon	1334-1434, 1549; Coleridge 1670; Sandford 1775, 1783, 1790, 1793, 1800; Wembworthy 1779.
Dorset	Beaminster 1775; Corfe Castle 1790; Melbury Osmond 1800; Poole 1574; Puddleton 1724-25; 1801, 1811, 1821.
Essex	Bocking 1793; Colchester 1377; Harlow 1797; 1811, 1821, 1831.
Forfarshire	1801.
Gloucestershire	1608; Bristol 1695; Olveston 1742; Uley 1795.
Guernsey	1821.
Hampshire	1801, 1811, 1821, 1831.
Herefordshire	1680.
Hertfordshire	1801.
Huntingdonshire	1549; Diocese of Ely 1716-44; 1811.
Isle of Man	Douglas 1730.
Jersey	1750, 1806, 1815; St Lawrence 1788.
Kent	1334-1434; Canterbury (and Diocese) 1565; Goodnestone 1676; Hayes 1790; New Romney 1695; Ramsgate 1773, 1785, 1792; Sandwich 1571; Wingham Petty Div 1705; Wrotham 1676; 1801, 1811, 1821, 1831.
Lancashire	Lancaster 1784; 1801, 1821, 1831.
Lincolnshire	Swinderby 1771, 1791.
London*	1377, 1638, 1640, 1677, 1695; Diocese of 1705, 1723-48, 1765, 1766, 1780; 1801, 1811, 1821, 1831.
Middlesex	Ealing 1599; 1801, 1811, 1821.
Norfolk	Norwich 1570; 1801, 1811, 1821, 1831.

Northamptonshire	Aynho 1740; Cogenhoe 1618-1628; Courteenhall 1587.
Nottinghamshire	1549; Clayworth 1676, 1688; West Retford 1794; 1821.
Orkney Isles	1821.
Oxfordshire	1549; Cuxham 1772; Kidlington 1545; Oxford 1377; Summertown 1832; 1801, 1811, 1821, 1831.
Renfrewshire	1695.
Shropshire	1821, 1831.
Somerset	Frome 1785; 1801.
Staffordshire	Archdeaconry 1532; Biddulph 1779; Stafford 1622; Stoke-upon-Trent 1701; 1801, 1811, 1821, 1831.
Suffolk	1801, 1821, 1831.
Surrey	1801, 1811, 1821, 1831.
Sussex	1297, 1334-1434; Rye 1488; 1811, 1821, 1831.
Warwickshire	Chilvers Coton 1684; Coventry 1523; Fenny Compton 1698; Stratford-on-Avon 1765; 1801, 1811, 1821, 1831.
Westmorland	1787.
Wigtownshire & Minnigaff	1684.
Wiltshire	Bowerchalke 1834-36; Box 1686; Cheverall, Little 1785; Chisleden 1787; Colerne 1774; Corsham 1770; Ditchridge 1686; Donhead 1695; Haslebury 1686; Marlborough 1600, 1601; Stanton St Bernard 1744; Steeple Ashton 1770; Swindon 1673; 1801, 1811, 1821, 1831.
Worcestershire	Worcester St Andrew 1795; 1831.

Yorkshire   1549; Diocese of York 1736; Hull 1377;
                                   York 1272, 1559, 1680 [15]; 1801, 1811, 1821, 1831.

---

* Normally refers to the City of London, although Westminster may also be included.

Appendix II - Decennial census returns from 1801 to 1831 with names and other details of individuals

1801

Berkshire	Binfield	CRO Reading
	Brightwell	CRO Reading
Buckinghamshire	Iver	CRO Aylesbury
Cambridgeshire	Cambridge, St Edward	CRO Cambridge
	Cambridge, St Mary the Great	CRO Cambridge
	Girton	CRO Cambridge
	Little Wilbraham	CRO Cambridge
Cheshire	Winwick with Hulme	Warrington Libry
Derbyshire	Clowne	CRO Matlock
Dorset	Oborne	County Record Office
	Sturminster Newton	County Record Office
	Winterbourne St Martin	County Record Office
Forfarshire	Dundee	Arch Rec Cen Dundee
Hampshire	Exton	CRO Winchester
	Fordingbridge	CRO Winchester
	Lymington	CRO Winchester
Hertfordshire	Barkway and Reed	County Record Office
	Hitchin	County Record Office
Kent	Borden	Ken Arch Off Maidstn
	Bromley	Bromley Centrl Libry
	Folkestone	Folkestone Ref Libry
	West Malling	Ken Arch Off Maidstn

	Smarden	Ken Arch Off Maidstn
Lancashire	Edgeworth	Manch & Lancs FHS
	Elton	CRO Preston
	Liverpool	City Record Office
	Winwick with Hulme	Warrington Libry
London, City of	St Helen Bishopgate	Guildhall Libry MSS
	St Nicholas Acons	Guildhall Libry MSS
	St Sepulchre	Guildhall Libry MSS
Middlesex	Chiswick	Chiswick Libry
	Chelsea St Luke	Chelsea Ref Libry
	Hampstead	Swiss Cottage Libry
	Hendon	Barnet Libry Hendon
	St James Piccadilly	Westminster City Lib
	St Mary le Strand	Westminster City Lib
Norfolk	Baconsthorpe	CRO Norwich
	Thorpe Episcopi (next Norwich)	CRO Norwich
	Winfarthing	CRO Norwich
	Woodton	CRO Norwich
Oxfordshire	Stonesfield	CRO Oxford
Somerset	Radstock	County Record Office
Staffordshire	Biddulph	CRO Stafford
	Walsall	Walsall Loc Hist Ctr
	Wednesbury	Wednesbury Distr Lib
Suffolk	Ipswich, St Peter	County Record Office
Surrey	Bletchingley	CRO Kingston
	Chobham	CRO Kingston
	Clapham	Gtr. Lnd. Record Office
	Ewhurst	CRO Kingston
	Guildford	Guildford Munt Rm
	Mortlake	CRO Kingston
	Newdigate	Guildford Munt Rm
	Nutfield	CRO Kingston
	Oxted	CRO Kingston
Warwickshire	Brinklow	CRO Warwick
	Church Lawford	CRO Warwick

Wiltshire	Box	CRO Trowbridge
Yorkshire	Bracewell	Leeds Distr Archives
	Elland-cum-Greetland	Calderdale Lib Halfx
	Hipperholme-cumBrighouse	Calderdale Lib Halfx
	Leeds (township - part)	Leeds Distr Archives
	Spofforth	Leeds Distr Archives
	Tong	Bradford Dist Archvs

1811

Bedfordshire	Kensworth	CRO Bedford
Berkshire	Brightwell	CRO Reading
	Comner	CRO Reading
Buckinghamshire	Lathbury (draft only)	CRO Aylesbury
Cambridgeshire	Balsham	CRO Cambridge
	Cambridge, St Edward	CRO Cambridge
	Cambridge, St Mary the Great	CRO Cambridge
	Ely St Mary	CRO Cambridge
	Trumpington	CRO Cambridge
Cheshire	Alderley	CRO Chester
Dorset	Whitchurch Canonicorum (part)	County Record Office
Essex	Ardleigh	CRO Chelmsford
	Horndon on the Hill	CRO Chelmsford
	Mundon	CRO Chelmsford
	Walthamstow	Vestry Ho Mus Whmstw
Hampshire	Fordingbridge	CRO Winchester
	Lymington	CRO Winchester
Huntingdonshire	Alwalton	CRO Huntingdon
Kent	Borden	Ken Arch Off Maidstn
	Goudhurst	Ken Arch Off Maidstn
	Luddesdown	Ken Arch Off Maidstn
	Smarden	Ken Arch Off Maidstn
London, City of	Allhallows Lombard Street	Guildhall Libry MSS
	St Ann Blackfriars (part)	Guildhall Libry MSS
	St Benet Paul's Wharf	Guildhall Libry MSS

	St Benet Sherhog	Guildhall Libry MSS
	St Botolph Bishopsgate	Guildhall Libry MSS
	St Jn the Bap upon Walbrook	Guildhall Libry MSS
	St Mary Woolchurch Haw	Guildhall Libry MSS
	St Mary Woolnorth	Guildhall Libry MSS
	St Nicholas Acons	Guildhall Libry MSS
	St Peter Paul's Wharf	Guildhall Libry MSS
	St Sepulchre	Guildhall Libry MSS
	St Swithin London Stone	Guildhall Libry MSS
	St Thomas Apostle	Guildhall Libry MSS
Middlesex	Hendon	Barnet Libry Hendon
	St John at Hackney*	Rose Lipman Libry
	Hampstead	Swiss Cottage Libry
	St Mary le Strand	Westminster City Libry
Norfolk	Baconsthorpe	CRO Norwich
	Great Bircham	CRO Norwich
	Winfarthing	CRO Norwich
Oxfordshire	Stonesfield	CRO Oxford
Staffordshire	Walsall	Walsall Loc Hist Ctr
	Wednesbury	Wednesbury Distr Lib
Surrey	Bletchingly	CRO Kingston
	Chobham	CRO Kingston
	Clapham	Gtr. Lnd. Record Office
	Croydon	Croydon Public Libry
	Mitcham	CRO Kingston
	Mortlake	CRO Kingston
	Newington	Gtr. Lnd. Record Office
	Nutfield	CRO Kingston
	Oxted	CRO Kingston
	Southwark St Saviour	Sthwk Loc Std Library
	Stoke d'Abernon	CRO Kingston
Sussex	East Grinstead**	CRO Chichester
	East Hoathly	County Record Office
	Hurstpierpoint**	CRO Chichester
	Kirdford**	County Record Office
	Rusper**	CRO Chichester
Warwickshire	Barston	CRO Warwick
	Warwick, St Mary	CRO Warwick

Wiltshire	Woodborough	County Record Office
Yorkshire	Calverley	Leeds Distr Archives
	Carleton in Craven	Leeds Distr Archives
	Elland-cum-Greetland	Calderdale Lib Halfx
	Farsley	Leeds Distr Archives
	Hipperholme-cum-Brighouse	Calderdale Lib Halfx
	Honley	Huddersfield Cen Lib
	Midgley	Calderdale Lib Halfx
	Sowerby	Calderdale Lib Halfx
	Tong	Bradford Dist Archiv
	Yeadon	Leeds Distr Archives

1821

Bedfordshire	Bedford, St Peter	Bedford Cen Library
	Blunham	CRO Bedford
	Haynes	CRO Bedford
Berkshire	Caversham	CRO Reading
	Earley	CRO Reading
Buckinghamshire	Chesham (part)	CRO Aylesbury
	Chenies (draft only - prob 1821)	CRO Aylesbury
	Iver (prob 1821)	CRO Aylesbury
	Princes Risborough	CRO Aylesbury
Cambridgeshire	Cambridge, St Benedict	CRO Cambridge
Cheshire	Alderley	CRO Chester
	Rosthern	CRO Cheshire
Dorset	Compton Abbas	County Record Office
	Horton	County Record Office
	Marnhull	County Record Office
	Shaftesbury St James	County Record Office
	Thornford	County Record Office
	Woodlands	County Record Office
Essex	Ardleigh	County Record Office
	Braintree	County Record Office
	Finchingfield	County Record Office
	Leyton	Vestry Ho Mus Wthstw
	Mistley	CRO Colchester
	Walthamstow	Vestry Ho Mus Wthstw
	Writtle	CRO Chelmsford

Guernsey	The Vale	Vale Douzaine
Hampshire	Fordingbridge	CRO Winchester
Kent	Beckenham	Bromley Centrl Libry
Lancashire	Penketh	Warrington Libry
London, City of	Allhallows Lombard Street	Guildhall Libry MSS
	St Benet Paul's Wharf	Guildhall Libry MSS
	St Benet Sherehog	Guildhall Libry MSS
	St Helen Bishopsgate	Guildhall Libry MSS
	St Katherine Coleman	Guildhall Libry MSS
	St Margaret Lothbury	Guildhall Libry MSS
	St Mary Woolchurch Haw	Guildhall Libry MSS
	St Mary Woolnoth	Guildhall Libry MSS
	St Nicholas Acons	Guildhall Libry MSS
	St Sepulchre	Guildhall Libry MSS
	St Swithin London Stone	Guildhall Libry MSS
	St Thomas Apostle	Guildhall Libry MSS
Middlesex	Hendon	Barnet Libry Hendon
	St Mary le Strand	Westminster City Libry
	St Marylebone	Marylebone Libry
	Poplar All Saints	Tower Hamlets Libry
Norfolk	Baconsthorpe	CRO Norwich
	Diss	CRO Norwich
	Dunston	CRO Norwich
	West Harling	CRO Norwich
	Sparham	CRO Norwich
	Winfarthing	CRO Norwich
	Wormegay	CRO Norwich
Nottinghamshire	Old and New Radford	County Record Office
Orkney Isles	Deerness	Kirkwall Libry
	Orphir	Kirkwall Libry
	St. Andrews	Kirkwall Libry
	Sandwick	Kirkwall Libry
	South Ronaldsay and Burray	Kirkwall Libry
	Stromness	Kirkwall Libry
Oxfordshire	Kiddington	CRO Oxford
	Stonesfield**	CRO Oxford

Shropshire	Shrewsbury Holy Cross & St Giles	County Lib Shrewsbry
Staffordshire	Walsall	Walsall Loc Hist Ctr
	Wednesbury	Wednesbury Distr Lib
Suffolk	Lowestoft	CRO Lowestoft
Surrey	Clapham	Gtr. Lnd. Record Office
	Mortlake	CRO Kingston
	Oxted	CRO Kingston
	Southwark Christch	Gtr. Lnd. Record Office
	Thursley	CRO Kingston
Sussex	East Grinstead	CRO Chichester
	Greatham	CRO Chichester
	Hurstpierpoint	CRO Chichester
Warwickshire	Austrey	County Record Office
	Barston	CRO Warwick
	Bedworth	County Record Office
	Farnborough	CRO Warwick
	Kineton	CRO Warwick
	Rugby	Rugby Library
	Tamworth	County Record Office
	Warwick, St Mary	CRO Warwick
Wiltshire	Stratford sub Castle	CRO Trowbridge
Yorkshire	Ossett cum Gawthorpe	Wakefield Library
	Spofforth	Leeds Distr Archives
	Thurstonland	Huddersfield Cen Lib
	Tong	Bradford Dist Archvs
	Warley	Calderdale Lib Halfx
	Yeadon	Leeds Distr Archives

1831

Bedfordshire	Ampthill	CRO Bedford
	Bedford, St Mary	CRO Bedford
	Ravensden	CRO Bedford
	Silsoe	CRO Bedford
Berkshire	Sellingford	CRO Reading
Buckinghamshire	Princes Risborough	CRO Aylesbury

Derry	entire county	Yth & Cmty Cen Derry
Essex	Finchingfield	CRO Chelmsford
	Ingatestone	CRO Chelmsford
	Leyton	Vestry Ho Mus Wthstw
	Mundon	CRO Chelmsford
	Steeple Bumpstead	CRO Chelmsford
	Walthamstow	Vestry Ho Mus Wthstw
Hampshire	Fordingbridge	CRO Winchester
Kent	Tenterden	Ken Arch Off Maidstn
Lancashire	Penketh	Warrington Libry
London, City of	St Benet Paul's Wharf	Guildhall Libry MSS
	St Christopher-le-Stocks	Guildhall Libry MSS
	St Katherine Cree	Guildhall Libry MSS
	St Margaret Lothbury	Guildhall Libry MSS
	St Mary Woolchurch Haw	Guildhall Libry MSS
	St Mary Woolnoth	Guildhall Libry MSS
	St Matthew Friday Street	Guildhall Libry MSS
	St Nicholas Acons	Guildhall Libry MSS
	St Peter Paul's Wharf	Guildhall Libry MSS
	St Peter Westcheap	Guildhall Libry MSS
	St Thomas Apostle	Guildhall Libry MSS
Middlesex	St John at Hackney**	Rose Lipman Library
	St Marylebone	Marylebone Library
	Poplar All Saints	Tower Hamlets Library
Norfolk	Alderford	CRO Norwich
	Coston	CRO Norwich
	Norwich St John de Sepulchre	CRO Norwich
	St Peter Southgate	CRO Norwich
Oxfordshire	Stonesfield	CRO Oxford
Shropshire	Bishops Castle (borough only)	CRO Shrewsbury
Staffordshire	Walsall	Walsall Loc Hist Ctr
Suffolk	Ipswich, St Margaret	CRO Ipswich
	Ipswich, St Peter	CRO Ipswich
	Lowestoft	CRO Lowestoft

Surrey	Abinger	CRO Kingston
	Banstead	CRO Kingston
	Chobham	CRO Kingston
	Merstham	CRO Kingston
	Newington	Sthwk Loc Std Library
	Nutfield	CRO Kingston
	Oxted	CRO Kingston
	Southwark, St Saviour	Sthwk Loc Std Library
	Streatham	Minet Library Lambeth
	Stoke d'Abernon	CRO Kingston
Sussex	East Grinstead	CRO Chichester
	Wisborough Green***	
Warwickshire	Astley	CRO Warwick
	Bidford	CRO Warwick
	Stratford-upon-Avon	Shksp Bplce Trst SuA
	Warwick, St Mary	CRO Warwick
Wiltshire	Bromham	CRO Trowbridge
Worcestershire	Wolverley	CRO Worcester
Yorkshire	Spofforth	Leeds Distr Archives
	Yeadon	Leeds Distr Archives

---

* heads of households and their occupations only

** heads of households only

*** Only the rector and lord of the manor are named

Notes & references

1. Numbers I. vv 1-54.

2. A villein had an interest in 60 acres and owned 4 oxen. A bordar had an interest in 15-30 acres and owned 2 oxen. A serf had an interest in 5 acres and owned 1 ox. A ploughland was the area which a ploughteam (8 oxen) could plough in an agricultural year; this amounted to approximately 120 acres but obviously depended on the terrain.

3. eg Hilary Jenkinson, Mrs (formerly V Rickards, Miss). 'An Early Bedfordshire Taxation (1237)'. Bdf Hist Rec Soc. Vol 2. (1914) p 225

4. ed F Collins. 'Register of the Freemen of the City of York. Vol I. 1272-1558'. Surtees Soc. Vol 96. (1896).

5. In 1290, 1294, 1295, 1296, 1297, 1301, 1306, 1307, 1309, 1313, 1315, 1319, 1322, 1327, 1332; See also: Beds Hist Rec Soc. Vol 39.(1959) for a typical 1297 account and also: M W Beresford. Amateur Historian. Vol 3 No 8. (1958) pp 325-328.

6. Ref: E 179 series; see also: M W Beresford. Amateur Historian. Vol 4 No 3. (1959) pp 101-109.

7. In East Sussex Record Office.

8. In Coventry City Record Office; see also: VCH Warwickshire Vol 8 p 4.

9. Ref: E 36 and E 315 series.

10. J R Western. 'The English Militia in the Eighteenth Century, 1660-1802'. (1965);and Lindsay Boynton. 'The Elizabethan Militia 1558-1638'. (1967).

11. In Amateur Historian. Vol 4 No 3. (1959) p 104.

12. Ed Ann J Kettle. 'A List of Families in the Archdeaconry of Stafford 1532-3'. Staffordshire Record Society. 4th series. Vol 8. (1976).

13. In Vol 8. Part IV. (May 1937) pp 359-363.

14. Ref: E 179/99/315 (Dev); E 179/122/143, 144, 146 (Hun); E 179/159/78, 182, 185 (Ntt); E 179/162/275 (Oxf); E179/203/251 (Ery); E 179/213/209 (Nry); E 179/208/211 (Wry); see also: M W Beresford. 'The Poll Tax and Census of Sheep 1549'. Agr Hist Rev. Vol i. (1953) pp 9-15; and Vol ii (1954) pp 15-29.

15. Ed F Collins. 'Register of the Freemen of the City of York. Vol II. 1559-1759'. Surtees Soc. Vol 102. (1899). An even more useful 'Register of York Freemen 1680 to 1986', with indexes to Freemen, Apprentices and Masters on microfiche, was compiled in 1989 by John Malden; publisher Wm Sessions Ltd, York.

16. Ref: Harl MS. 594-5.

17. Kent Record Office; the Canterbury parishes are ref: E/Q/1 (only parts of St. Martin and St. Paul survive); the Diocesan Communicants Lists are ref: PRC 43/13/12.

18. Ed J F Pound. Norfolk Record Society. Vol 40. (1971) p 28.

19. Calendar State Papers. Vol 78. 29 Domestic. Elizabeth. 1547-80. p 414

20. In E 377/1, 2, 3 & 4 and SP 12/142/33, 12/183/15, 12/200/61 etc; see also: D J Steel. 'Sources for Roman Catholic and Jewish Genealogy and Family History'. (1974).

21. For example: Roll No 1 1592-3 in Cath Rec Soc. Vol 18. (1916); Roll No 2 1593-4 in Cath Rec Soc. Vol 57. (1965); Roll No 3 1594-5 in Cath Rec Soc. Vol 61. (1970); Roll No 4 1595-6 with Roll No 3.

22. Ref: 86 P/6.

23. Ref: E 179 220/150.

24. Bull Bd Cel Stud. Vol 8. Pt IV. (May 1937) pp 336-343.

25. In E 163/24/35; see also: K J Allison. 'An Elizabethan Village Census'. Ealing LHS. Members Papers. No 2. (Oct 1962); and also: Bulletin of the Inst of Hist Research. Vol 36. No 93. (May 1963) pp 91-103.

26. Ref: Harl MS. Vol 280. ff 157-172.

27. eg C W Forster 'The State of the Church in the reigns of Elizabeth and James I as illustrated by documents relating to the Diocese of Lincoln. Vol I'. Lincoln Rec Soc. Vol 23. (1926) pp 253-353.

28. A J & R H Tawney. Econ Hist Rev. Vol V. No 1. (Oct 1934) pp 25-64.

29. G H Dury. 'The Population of Guernsey: An Essay in Historical Geography'. Geog. Vol 33. (1948) pp 61-69; see also: C A Robin. 'Notes on the Population of Guernsey'. (1947).

30. Ref: WS.L.D. 1721/1/4.

31. S O Addy. Dby Arch & Nat Hist Soc. Vol VI. (Jan 1884) pp 49-74.

32. Fifth Report of the Royal Commission on Historical Manuscripts, Pt I. Report & Appendix. (1876) pp 3 and 120-134; see also: Wilts Notes and Queries. Vol 7. (1911-13) pp 16-21, 79-84, 105-110, 162-167, 203-208, 260-265, 309-313, 343-347, 418-421, 450-452, 496-499; and also: Society of Genealogists' Leaflet. No 8. 'The Protestation Returns of 1641-2'.

33. J S W Gibson. 'The Hearth Tax and Later Stuart Tax Lists and the Association Oath Rolls'. Fed of Fam Hist Socs. (2nd edn 1986).

34. Ref: H/2.

35. Ref: MS 639 and VPIC/9.

36. Ref: MS.Salt 33. [formerly catalogued as No 2112].

37. T Richards. 'The Religious Census of 1676; An Inquiry into its Historical Value, Mainly in Reference to Wales'. Trans Hon Soc of Cym. (1927) Supp pp 1-118; [pp 1-15 are generic].

38. E A Whiteman. 'The Compton Census of 1676: a critical edition' Rec Soc & Econ Hist. New Series. Vol 10 (1986).

39. Kent Records. Vol 17. (1960) pp 153-174;

40. Mary J Dobson. 'Original Compton Census Returns: The Shoreham Deanery'. Archaeologia Cantiana. Vol 94. (1978) pp 61-73.

41. In Transactions of the Cumberland and Westmoreland Antiquarian and Archaeological Society. Vol 51. New Series. (1952). Article 13 pp 137-141.

42. A S Langley. 'A Religious Census of 1676 AD'. Lin Notes & Queries. Vol 16. No 2. (April 1920) pp 33-51.

43. E L Guilford. 'Nottinghamshire in 1676'. Trans Thoroton Soc. Vol 28. (1924) pp 106-113; [transcribed from the Tanner MSS. (150 ff 28 and 129) in the Bodleian Library, Oxford].

44. D P Dymond. 'Suffolk and the Compton Census of 1676'. Suffolk Review. Vol 3. (1966) pp 103-118.

45. (Rev D Bond). 'The Compton Census - Peterborough'. Local Population Studies. Vol X. (1973) pp 71-74; but only six parish enumerations have been transcribed for this brief article.

46. P Laslett and J Harrison. 'Clayworth and Cogenhoe'; in Historical Essays Presented to David Ogg. ed H E Bell and R L Ollard. (1963) pp 157-184; see also: P Laslett. 'The World We Have Lost'. (1965).

47. Ed H Gill and E L Guilford. 'The Rector's Book of Clayworth, Nottinghamshire'. (1910) pp 84-87.

48. CWF Goss. 'The London Directories, 1677-1855'. (1932).

49. Jane E Norton. 'Guide to the National and Provincial Directories of England and Wales, excluding London, published before 1856'. (1950). 2nd edn 1984.

50. Main Papers 3 Dec 1680 No 321; as identified in Hist Man Com Vol XI. pt ii. (1887) pp 222-237.

51. ed W Scott. 'Parish Lists of Wigtownshire and Minnigaff'. Scot Rec Soc. Vol 50. (1916).

52. Dr Richard Price. 'Observations on Reversionary Payments on Schemes for Providing Annuities for Widows, and for Persons in Old Age; on the Method of Calculating the Values of Assurance on Lives; and on the National Debt'. (6th ed 1806). ed William Morgan. Vol 2. p 27 (footnote). This edition contains a number of typographical errors which were not present in the tables when they first appeared in his 'Essay on the Population of England from the Revolution to the Present Time' in 1780. The 1st edn of 'Observations' was published in 1771; as Price died in 1791 the last edition to which he personally made additions or corrections was the 5th, published in 1792. There was a 7th edn in 1812 to which population scholars often allude but the references in this cameo are taken from my own copy of Price's 'Observations'. Volume 1 of his 'Observations' deals mostly with life expectancy data whereas volume 2 discusses population figures. All the references in this cameo are taken from volume 2.

53. By F Beckwith in 'The Population of Leeds during the Industrial Revolution'. Thoresby Soc. Vol 41. (1954). Miscellany. Vol 12. Pt 2. (1948) p 121 footnote 4.

54. at the Guildhall, London; see also: E Jones & A V Judges. 'London Population in the late 17th Century'. Econ Hist Rev. Vol VI. No 1. (Oct 1935) pp 45-63.

55. P H Styles. 'A census of a Warwickshire Village in 1698'. Univ of Birmingham Hist Jour. Vol 3. No 1. (1951) pp 33-51; and in general: E A Wrigley. 'An Introduction to English Historical Demography'. (1966).

56. R E Chester Waters. 'A Statutory List of the Inhabitants of Melbourne, Derbyshire in 1695'. Jour Dby Arch & Nat Hist Soc. Vol 7. (June 1885) pp 4-30.

57. C R Webb. 'The Association Oath Rolls of 1695'. Genealogists' Magazine. Vol 21. No 4. (Dec 1983) pp 120-123; see also : original rolls at PRO, Chancery Lane in Class C 213.

58. eg D V Glass and D E C Eversley. 'Population in History'. (1965).

59. K Walton. 'The Distribution of Population in Aberdeenshire'. Scot Geog Mag. Vol 66. No 1. (June 1950) pp 17-26.

60. The full title is: 'Philosophical Transactions, giving some account of the Present Undertakings, Studies and Labours, of the ingenious in many considerable parts of the world'. It comprised papers often written by one party and then "communicated" via a second party to the Royal Society and subsequently read at meetings of its members prior to publication. A volume issued for one particular year was often not published until the subsequent year and hence some modern authors quote different dates for the same reference. In this cameo the year for which, and not in which, the volume was issued is quoted and hereafter the publication is abbreviated to 'Philosophical Transactions' or, in these notes, to Phil Tran Roy Soc. see: Phil Tran Roy Soc. Vol 22. (1700) pp 520-524; see also: Price. Op cit. p 23 (footnote) for Dublin; p 176 (footnote) for Maidstone.

61. see: R Talbot. 'Fenton'. Stoke on Trent. (1977) pp 22-28.

62. J Collinson. 'History and antiquities of the County of Somerset, collected from records made by Edmund Rack'. (1791). Vol 2 p27.

63. Main Papers 1 Mar 1706 No 2249b. Calendared in Manuscripts of the House of Lords. Vol 6. (New Series). (1704-1706) pp 417-421.

64. see also: G Huelin. 'Some 18th Century Roman Catholic Recusants' Jour of Eccl Hist Vol VII. No 1. (April 1956) pp 61-68; and also: P Coverdale. 'Essex Papists in 1706'. Essex Recusant. No 2. Vol 1. (1960) pp 16-29.

65. Main Papers 1 Mar 1706 No 2249c. Calendared in Manuscripts of the House of Lords. Vol 6. (New Series). (1704-1706) pp 421-423.

66. see also: E S Worrall. Essex Recusant. Vol 2. (1960) p 88.

67. eg in Wilts Rec Off, Trowbridge; formerly in the Diocesan Archives at Salisbury, ref: 'Returns of Papists'; see also: Recusant History. Vol 7. No 1. (Jan 1963).

68. eg for York Diocese in Cath Rec Soc. Vol 32. (1932) p 350.

69. ref: MS. 9550.

70. L Munby. 'Hertfordfordshire Population Statistics, 1563-1801'. (1964).

71. ref: Bowtell's draft for 'A History of Cambridge'. Vol 3 p 355.

72. C H Cooper. 'Annals of Cambridge'. (1852). Vol 4.

73. Manx Soc. Vol 30. 3rd article. (1880).

74. Cath Rec Soc. Vol 32. (1932) p 204; see also: Cath Rec Soc. Vol 4. (1907) pp 368-373; and also: Northern Genealogist. Vol III. (1900) pp 84-88.

75. J Hunter. 'Hallamshire'. (1819) p 21; the correct title is 'The History and Topography of the Parish of Sheffield in the County of York with Historical and descriptive Notices of the parishes of Ecclesfield, Hamsworth, Treeton and Whiston, and the Chapelry of Bradfield'; there were 'New and Enlarged' editions in 1869 and 1882 by Rev Alfred Gatty, vicar of Ecclesfield and Sub-dean of York.

76. Rare Book Dept Add. 2766(15).7500.2.1./25; [St Helier and St Ouen are missing].

77. Phil Tran Roy Soc. Vol 48. (1754) pp 788-800; Vol 49. (1756) pp 877-890; Vol 50. (1757) pp 465-479; see also: W Maitland. 'History of London....'. (1739) pp 533-542;[later editions were in 1756, 1772 and 1775]; and also: R Price. Op cit. pp 20, 21, 24 (footnotes) and 141.

78. P Morant. 'History and antiquities of the County of Essex....'. (1768). Vol 2 p 1.

79. W Maitland. 'History of Edinburgh from its foundation to the present time....Together with the ancient and present state of the town of Leith, etc.'. 1753. p 171.

80. R Price. Op cit. pp 57, 72 and 107.

81. ref: MS. Top. Glouc. c 4-5.

82. T D Fosbroke. 'An Original History of the City of Gloucester....including also the original papers of....R Bigland'.(1819) p193.

83. Vols 71, 72, 75, 77.

84. R Price. Op cit. pp 70, 94, 95, 101 and 113.

85. in 'Parliamentary Papers - Reports for Commissioners - Registrar General'. (Session 1847-8). Vol 25 pp 289-325.

86. Gentlemen's Magazine. Vol 17. (1747) p 326.

87. W Maitland. Op cit. pp 217-218.

88. R Price. Op cit. p 57.

89. E Carter. 'The History of the County of Cambridge from the earliest account to the Present Time'. (1753). pp 14-45.

90. ref: P25/28/1-2.

91. ref: Gough, Cambs, 76.

92. ref: CO 217. Vol 9 pp 226-227.

93. Cha Isl FH Jour. No 38. (Spring 1988) pp 180-184.

94. R Price. Op cit. pp 34, 35, 70, 100, 101, 106 and 397; see also: Phil Tran Roy Soc. Vol 52. (1761) pp 140-141; Vol 61. (1771) pp 57-58; Vol 72. (1782) pp 53-57.

95. Phil Tran Roy Soc. Vol 48. (1753) pp 217-220.

96. R Price. Op cit. pp 70 and 100.

97. I Chronicles. XXI. vv 1-17.

98. eg H Heginbotham. 'Stockport: Ancient and Modern'. (1892) p 87. and Rev J Watson. 'A manuscript collection towards the History of Cheshire'. (1783). Vol 1 p 129.

99. ed J G Kyd. Scot Hist Soc. Third Series. Vol 44. (1952).

100. R Price. Op cit. p 21 (footnote).

101. Population Studies. Vol 15. (1961-2) pp 198-200;

102. Phil Tran Roy Soc. Vol 48. (1755) pp 788-799.

103. Add MSS 4440 ff 176 et seq.

104. R Price. Op cit. p 204 (footnote).

105. William Wales. 'An Inquiry into the Present State of Population in England and Wales; and the Proportion Which the present Number of Inhabitants bears to the Number at former Periods'. (1781) p 67.

106. R Price. Op cit. pp 220 and 238.

107. R Price. Op cit. p 40 (footnote).

108. Phil Tran Roy Soc. Vol 64. (1774) pp 54-66.

109. R B Wheler.'History and antiquities of Stratford upon Avon, comprising....'. (1806) pp 16-17.

110. see also: D J Steel.'Sources for Roman Catholic and Jewish Genealogy and Family History'. (1974) p 908.

111. R Price. Op cit. pp 35, 70, 220 and 239.

112. House of Lords Rec Off. Main Papers 21 Dec 1767. [Not calendared]; see also: Catholic Ancestor. Vol 3. No 1. (Feb 1990) pp 22-26; and also: D J Steel. Op cit. pp 908-909.

113. R Price. Op cit. pp 40 (footnote), 70 and 72; see also: W Money. 'History of the ancient town and borough of....Newbury, Berks....'. (1887) p 571.

114. R Price. Op cit. p 43 (footnote) for Okeford; pp 70 and 174 (footnote) for Birmingham; p 71 for Bury.

115. R Price. Op cit. pp 70 and 71.

116. ref: Swinderby par. 23/1.

117. R Price. Op cit. pp 43 (footnote) and 70.

118. F Beckwith. 'The Population of Leeds during the Industrial Revolution'. Thoresby Soc. Vol 41. (1954). Miscellany. Vol 12. Pt 2. (1948) pp 118-196 and 401; see also: R Price. Op cit. pp 70 and 225 (footnote).

119. Phil Tran Roy Soc. Vol 64. (1774) pp 62-63.

120. R Price. Op cit. p 13 (footnote).

121. R Price. Op cit. p 70.

122. Phil Tran Roy Soc. Vol 64. (1774) pp 67-78. The Altringham figures for families and inhabitants were also quoted by Price in his 'Observations' p 70; in quoting the Chester survey of houses, families and inhabitants, he states 'St Michael's parish: Op cit. p 71; see also: R Price. Op cit. p 70 for Chester in 1774.

123. Phil Tran Roy Soc. Vol 68. (1778) pp 131-154.

124. R Price. Op cit. p 70 for Bolton and Little Bolton; p 23 (footnote), p 70, pp 216 and 227 (footnotes) for Manchester and Salford; p 71 for Chippenham; p 224 (footnote) for Horwick, Darwent, Cockey Moor and Chowbent; see also: Phil Tran Roy Soc. Vol 65 (1775).

125. Phil Tran Roy Soc. Vol 64. (1774) pp 438-444.

126. Phil Tran Roy Soc. Vol 68. (1778) pp 615-621.

127. T R Nash. 'Collections for the history of Worcestershire'. Vol 2. (1781-1799) pp 40 and 278-279.

128. Dr W Enfield. 'An Essay towards the history of Leverpool drawn up from papers left by the late Mr George Perry'. (2nd edn 1774) pp 23-24. [Price also quoted generously from Enfield's data].

129. Phil Tran Roy Soc. Vol 64. (1774) p 57; [taken from p 28 of the second edn of Enfield's 'History of Leverpool'].

130. W Boys. 'Collections for a History of Sandwich in Kent, with notices of the other Cinque ports....and of Richborough'. (1792) p 832; and also: E Hasted. 'History and Topographical survey of the County of Kent'. Vol 10. 2nd edn. (1801) p 379.

131. ref: PO 13.

132. R Price. Op cit. p 71. Price referred to the town as Wycombe.

133. Gentlemen's Magazine. Vol 70. (1800). Pt 2 p 1160; [the information is supplied in a letter of 12 Dec 1800 where the town is referred to by its contemporary name of Chipping Wycombe].

134. R Price. Op cit p 173 (footnote).

135. Phil Tran Roy Soc. Vol 64. (1774) pp 54-66; and Vol 65. (1775) pp 322-335; see also: R Price. Op cit. pp 72 and 216 (footnote).

136. Phil Tran Roy Soc. Vol 65. (1775) pp 424-445.

137. Phil Tran Roy Soc. Vol 66. (1776) pp 160-167.

138. R Price. Op cit. pp 71 and 224/5 (footnote) for Tattenhall and Waverton and p 72 for Bala.

139. R Price. Op cit. p 173 (footnote); see also: W Boys. Op cit. p 784.

140. R Price. Op cit. pp 168-170.

141. R Price. Op cit. p 72 and pp 106 and 107 (footnotes).

142. T R Nash. Op cit. Vol 2 p 411.

143. R Price. Op cit. pp 166-172.

144. In Bdf FHS Jour. Vol 6. No 3 (Autumn 1987) pp28-32.

145. R Price. Op cit. p 71.

146. ref: Argyll Estate Papers. 'List of Families residing on His Grace The Duke of Argylls Property in Kantyre....'. (1779); and 'Argyll Estates Census' (1792); [in volume with Chamberlain's Accounts and Kintyre Feu Duties. Deed Box. Rosneath No 8].

147. R A Gailey. 'Settlement and Population in Kyntyre 1750-1800'. Scot Geog Mag. Vol 76. No II. (Sep 1960) pp 99-107.

148. R Lowe. 'General View of the Agriculture of the County of Nottingham'. (2nd edn 1798). Appdx 12B pp 179-187; [1st edn was 1794]; see also: R Price. Op cit. p 70.

149. ref: D3539/1/48.

150. R Price. Op cit. pp 43 (footnote) and 70.

151. see also: T R Nash. Op cit. Vol 2. Appdx p cxvii.

152. ref: 1165 Z/Z 1.

153. ref: IR 23 (at Kew); see also: Brit Parl Pap. (1844). HC 619. Vol 32. 389.

154. W Wales. Op cit. p 67.

155. R Price. Op cit. p 169.

156. Main Papers 5 Mar 1781.

157. Vol 37. p 230.

158. see: D J Steel. Op cit. pp 909-910.

159. Dr J Aikin. 'A description of the country from thirty to forty miles round Manchester;

containing...'. (1795) p 304; R Price. Op cit. p 249 for Warrington [but on p 71 Price states this survey was made in April 1781]; R Price. Op cit. pp 71 and 175/176 (footnote) for Maidstone, 1781 and 1782.

160. R Price. Op cit. p 71 for Swindon.

161. VCH Wiltshire. Vol 8. (1965) p 93 for Warminster.

162. ref: HW 60-62.

163. R Price. Op cit. pp 204 and 205 (footnotes).

164. R Price. Op cit. pp 174 and 175 (footnotes).

165. Phil Tran Roy Soc. Vol 72. (1782) pp 35-43.

166. F M Eden.'The State of the Poor'. (1797). Vol 3 pp 750-751.

167. J Collinson. Op cit. Vol 2 pp 186 and 198.

168. F M Eden. Op cit. Vol 2 p 643.

169. H Lonsdale. 'The Life of Dr Heysham'. (1780).

170. W Hutchinson. 'History of Cumberland'. (1796). Vol 2 p 674.

171. Cha Isl FH Jour. Vols 8 (Autumn 1980) - 14 (Spring 1982).

172. J Pilkington. 'A View of the Present State of Derbyshire with an account of its most remarkable antiquities'. (2nd edn. 1803). Vol 2 p 338; [1st edn was 1789].

173. S Shaw. 'History and antiquities of Staffordshire, compiled from....including Erdeswick's Survey....'. (1798) p 12.

174. R Lowe. Op cit. pp 172-177.

175. M Dunsford. 'Historic Memoirs of the Town and Parish of Tiverton....'. (1790) p 464.

176. J Hutchins. 'The History and Antiquities of the County of Dorset'. (2nd edn. 1815). [1st edn was 1796]; see also: LPS No 22. Spring 1979 pp 14-29.

177. ref: U 468.

178. Dr J Toulmin 'History of Taunton in the County of Somersetshire'. (1791) pp 189-190.

179. J Toulmin 'Present State of Taunton'. Monthly Magazine and British Register. Vol 17. (1804) p 528.

180. ref: Swinderby par. 23/10.

181. J Ticknell. 'History of the Town and County of Kingston upon Hull'. (1796) p 854.

182. F M Eden. Op cit. Vol 3 p 827.

183. ref: DR 230/79

184. F M Eden. Op cit. Vol 3 pp 750-751.

185. J Brewster. 'Parochial History and Antiquities of Stockton upon Tees....including an account....'. (1829) pp 256-266.

186. C Wright. 'The Brighton Ambulator,containing historicaland topographical delineations of the town....'. (1818) p 102.

187. M Lloyd-Baker. 'The Story of Uley'. (c1910, ND) pp 49-58; [the first edition contained neither the map nor the list of names].

188. F M Eden. Op cit. Vol 3 p 705.

189. I F W Beckett. 'The Buckinghamshire Posse Commitatus, 1798'. Bkm Rec Soc. Vol 22. (1985); see also: Brit Mus Stowe MSS 805 and 806.

190. J Gibson & M Medlycott. 'Militia Lists and Musters 1757-1876'. Fed of Fam Hist Soc. (1989).

191. J James ed. 'Comyn's New Forest'. (1982).

192. D J Steel. 'General Sources of Births, Marriages and Deaths Before 1837'. (1976). p336.

193. ref: MS. Top OXON c 240.

194. ref: P 11/28/4.

There are regular articles on and references to censuses and enumerations in specialist journals such as 'Population Studies', 'Local Population Studies', and publications of the Cambridge Group for the History and Population and Social Structure, a unit of the Social Science Research Council. Each of these has assisted me in seeking examples of listings of one sort or another and with their continued publication will undoubtedly provide further examples as they come to light.